Alaska

MAGAZINE'S

Cabin Cookbook

Salmon Loaf   Page 15
Splender Spaghella   ,, 45
Rhubarb Crumble   ,, 89

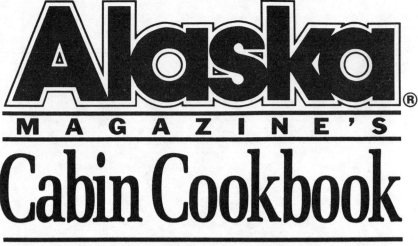

MAGAZINE'S
Cabin Cookbook

Over 150 favorite North Country recipes that tell how to cook with wild game, fish, fowl, and native plants.

By
The Old Homesteader
with Help from
A. Friend and An Other

Alaska Publishing Properties, Inc.
808 E Street, Suite 200
Anchorage, Alaska 99501

ISBN: 0-89909-186-5

ALASKA Magazine
is published monthly by

Alaska Publishing Properties, Inc.
808 E Street, Suite 200
Anchorage, Alaska 99501

Table of Contents

Foreword 9
The Ones That Didn't Get Away:
Halibut, Salmon, and Other Fish 11

Broiled Halibut 11
Beer Batter Halibut 11
Bounty of the Sea 12
Halibut Quiche 12
Baked Halibut with Shrimp Sauce 12
Nancy's Halibut Chowder . . 13
Stuffed Fished Rolls . . . 13
Stuffed Halibut Fillets . . . 13
Campfire Broiled Salmon . . 14
Seafood Salad 14
Baked Salmon 14
Salmon Loaf 15
Salmon Cakes 15
Salmon Sandwiches . . . 15
Salmon Croquettes 16
Grilled Salmon 16
Salmon Salad 16
Soft-Smoked Salmon . . . 17
Salmon Balls 17
Grayling Fry 17
Hooligan Fry 18
Nancy's Fish Stock 18
Flaked Fish Hash 19
Fish and Tomato Soup . . . 19
Tomato Poached Fish . . . 19
Oven-Fried Fish Fillets . . . 19
Salmon Patties with Spinach Sauce 20

Come Out of Your Shell:
Clams, Scallops, Shrimp,
and Crabs 21

Uncle Joe's Old-Fashioned
Clambake 21
Steamed Clams 22
Fried Clams 22
Clam Milk Stew 22
Clam Chowder 22
Clam Fritters 23
Scalloped Clams 23
Skillet Hash 23
Clam Gulch Clamburgers . . 24
Stuffed Clams 24
Shepherd's Clam Pie . . . 24
Clam Pan Roast 25
Clam Soufflé 25
Exotic Steamed Clams . . . 25
Seafood Chowder 25
Crab Cocktail 26
King Crab and Green Stuff . . 26
Alaska Deviled Crab . . . 26
Crab in Cheese Sauce . . . 27
Crab Cakes 27
Crab Picnic Buns 27
Crab Cakes Alaskan . . . 27
Crab Louis 28
Fried Scallops 28
Stir-Fried Scallops 28
Scallops en Casserole . . . 28

Seafood Dinner 29
Grilled Scallops 29
Layered Shrimp Salad . . . 29
Garlic Shrimp 30
Shrimp Stateside Style . . . 30
Hot Stuff 30
Eggs Again! 31

The Big Ones:
Moose, Caribou, Dall Sheep,
and Others **32**

Moose Noodle Soup 32
Alaskan Spaghetti 33
Pâté of Game Liver (Liver Spread) 33
Pepper Steak 33
Stock from Game 34
Roast in Foil 34
Caribou Swiss Steak 35
Bubble and Squeak 35
Green Pepper Caribou Steak . 35
Mooseburger with Onions . . 36
Chiliburgers Deluxe 36
Moose or Caribou Casserole Steak 36
Smothered Moose Flank Steak 37
Chili 37
Chicken-Fried Moose Steak . 38
Blind Pigeons 38
Cheesy Moose-Tomato Pie . . 38
Stuffed Heart 39
Kidneys in Tomato Sauce . . 39
Meatballs 39
Burger-Stuffed Peppers . . . 40
Crunchy Meatballs 40
Stuffed Flank Steak 41
Alaska Scrapple 41
Onion Soup 41
Gingered Game Strips . . . 42
Alaskan Broiled Steak . . . 42
Pan-Fried Moose Steak . . . 42
Sheep Mountains 43
Curried Mountain Sheep . . 43
Wild Game Chino 43
Braised Venison 44
German-Alaskan Potato Soup
with Dumplings 44
Splendid Spaghetti 45

Mooseburger Pizza 45
Campfire Barbecued Ribs . . 46
Mooseburger Lasagna 46
Mountain Man's Shish Kebabs . 47
Caribou Rump Roast 47
Roast Mountain Goat 47
Medium-Famous Orca Jones
Vegetable Mess 47
Venison Goulash 48
Moose Jambalaya 48
Meatball Soup 48
Mesquite Moose Steaks . . . 49
Burger Shortcake 49
Mooseburger Pudding . . . 49
Mixed Broil 50
Burger Loaf 50
Burger Balls 50
Moosibou Cakes 51
Broiled Gameburger Rolls . . 51
Snackeroo 51
Spanish Liver 52
Game Casserole 52
Sweet and Sour Black Bear . . 53
Roast Venison, Greek Style . . 53
Reindeer Pot Roast 53
Seal Casserole 54
Cooking Walrus Meat 54
Gameburger Gravy 54
Sauce 'n' Burger 54
Truly Delicious Gameburger
Casserole 55
Alaska Mincemeat 55
Mincemeat Drop Cookies . . 56
Layered Game Casserole . . . 56
Country-Style Meat Pie . . . 56
Meat Loaf Mix-Up 57

Feathers and Fur:
Game Birds and Rabbit . . . **58**

Spruce Chicken Juniper . . . 58
Marinated Spruce Grouse . . 58
Mulligatawny Soup 59
Wild Goose in Mushroom Sauce 59
Roast Wild Goose 59
Duck Stew with Dumplings . 60
Barbecued Wild Duck 60

Duck Surprise 61
Duck Casserole 61
Braised Grouse Breasts . . . 61
Baked Grouse or Ptarmigan . 62
Creamed Wild Fowl . . . 62
Wild Bird Casserole . . . 62
Ptarmigan Stir-Fry 62
Wild Fowl Soup 63
Brunswick Stew 63
Oven-Fried Rabbit 64
Smothered Rabbit 64

It's the Berries:
Wild Berries and Rose Hips . 65

Blueberry Muffins 65
Blueberry Salad 65
Blueberry Ginger Crisp . . 66
Blueberry Custard 66
Blueberry Parfait 66
Pop-in-a-Pan Pies 66
Double-Zip Blueberry Pie . . 67
Blueberry Pie 67
Berry-Banana Nuggets . . . 67
Blueberry Omelet 68
Alaskan Party Cheesecakes . . 68
Currant Jelly 69
Currant Sauce 69
Currant Jelly Sauce 69
Cranberry Punch 69
Cranberry Bread 70
Cranberry Chutney 70
Uncooked Cranberry Sauce . . 71
Wild Raspberry Cake . . . 71
Cloudberry Whip 71
Jam Rolls 71
Berry Pandowdy 72
Berry Mousse 72

Wild Berry Syrups 72
Wild Berry Shortcake . . . 73
Rose Hips (Rose Fruit) . . . 73
Juniper Sauce 73
Candied Rose Hips 74
Highbush Cranberry Catsup . 74

Just Weeds:
Edible Wild Plants
and Mushrooms 75

Freezing Mushrooms 75
Mushroom and Potato Pie . . 75
Alaska Salad 76
Mushroom Salad 76
Puffball Salad 76
Ham with Puffballs 77
Puffball Sauté 77
Mushroom Soup 77
Pan-Fried Morels 78
French-Fried Shaggy Mane
Mushrooms 78
New Potatoes with Chives . . 79
Cream of Chives Soup . . . 79
Chive Turnovers 79
Egg in a Nest 80
Fiddleheads 80
Spring Salad 80
Fireweed Salad 80
Goosetongue Greens 81
Wilted Wild Greens . . . 81

Sassy Sourdough:
Sourdough from Start to Finish 82

Basic Sourdough Starter . . . 82
Sourdough Bread 82
Sourdough Knots or Sticks . . 83
Buttermilk Sourdough Bread . 83
Sourdough Pan Rolls 84
Burger Buns 84
Sourdough French Bread . . . 85
Parker House Sourdough Rolls . 85
Sourdough Braids 85
Sourdough Hotcakes 86
Sourdough Waffles 86
Cinnamon Rolls 87

Pecan Rolls 87
Herbed French Bread . . . 87
Chocolate Cake 88
Sourdough Hermits . . . 88

Tail Ends:
Items That Don't Fit
Anywhere Else 89

Rhubarb Crumble 89
Rhubarb Conserve 89
Strawberry-Rhubarb Jam . . 89
Candied Rhubarb Pie . . . 90

Mat-Su Potatoes 90
Homestead Harvest 90
The Extraordinary Carrot . . 91
White Sauce 91
Corn Bread Stuffing . . . 91
Marinade for Wild Game . . 92
All-Purpose Marinade . . 92
Tartare Sauce for Seafood . . 92
Cream Gravy 93

Items to Keep on Hand . . . **94**

Glossary **95**

8

Foreword

No attempt has been made within this little book to cover all of Alaska's edibles. We have included just the dishes we most enjoy, with a few extra thrown in for variety and fun.

We want to emphasize here that you do not need to have access to Alaska's resources to use these recipes. Most game meat is interchangeable with meat from the butcher shop. Wild berries and supermarket berries can be substituted one for the other, of course. With mushrooms, however, one must be careful and really learn the edible ones from the others.

The more you experiment with different kinds of game and the more you vary the seasonings you use, the more fascinated you will become with the infinite possibilities of fish and game cookery.

Just remember this: There is no reason for anyone to say that he doesn't like wild game. If it is dressed correctly in the field, stored properly, and prepared for the table in an approved manner, it will not taste strong or "gamey" and should please anyone's palate. Above all, never overcook game or seafood.

In parting let us say that we are grateful to those people who shared their favorite recipes with us. Their contributions helped to make the book more interesting.

THE ONES THAT DIDN'T GET AWAY:
Halibut, Salmon, and Other Fish

Alaska has an enormous variety and abundance of fish in its fresh and coastal waters, and most Alaskans like fishing about as well as any sport. They don't do it entirely for sport, though. For most of us in the North, fish are an important part of our diet. The elements they provide are essential for good nutrition and, best of all, fish make for good eating.

BROILED HALIBUT

Rockfish or cod may be substituted for halibut, but since we have halibut more often in the freezer that is what we use. Actually, any white-meated fish would work just as well.

Combine ½ cup soy sauce, 4 or 5 tablespoons sherry, 1 large clove garlic, minced, ½ teaspoon ground ginger, and 2 teaspoons honey. Marinate 4 halibut steaks (about 6 or 7 ounces each) in this mixture for an hour. After 30 minutes turn the steaks over to be sure they are marinated equally on all sides. Remove from the marinade and drain. Place the steaks on a broiler pan — not touching each other — and broil them about 4 inches underneath the heating element. Broil about 10 minutes per inch of thickness, measured at the thickest part, or until the fish flakes when tested with a fork. Serve with lemon wedges and a small sprig of parsley.

BEER BATTER HALIBUT

We've found that good quality, light-colored beers work best. For this batter the flavor of dark beers is too strong.

Cut a couple of pounds of halibut into 1-inch-thick chunks. Heat cooking oil in a deep-fat fryer to 375°F. Make the batter by combining 1 cup flour, one 12-ounce bottle (or can) of beer, 1 tablespoon paprika, and 1½ teaspoons salt.

Dip the halibut in the batter and drop the pieces into the hot oil a few at a time. Cook the fish chunks until the batter is golden brown — just a few minutes. Halibut overcooks easily, so try not to overdo it. Remove the fish pieces from the oil and drain on paper towels; serve piping hot with your favorite accompaniments.

– John Sadusky

BOUNTY OF THE SEA

The Bounty is best made with fresh sea-food, but frozen or canned may also be used. This is a recipe created by Italian fishermen, who put in everything they harvested from the sea — hence the name. Feel free to make changes to suit your own taste.

Heat ¼ cup olive oil and 4 or 5 table-spoons margarine in a frying pan. Sauté 3 finely chopped cloves of garlic, 1¼ cups chopped onion, and 1 cup chopped green pepper. Transfer this mixture to a 6-quart pot and add one 28-ounce can tomatoes, one 6-ounce can tomato paste, 1 bay leaf, ⅓ cup chopped parsley, 2 teaspoons oregano, ½ teaspoon basil, 2 teaspoons sea salt, and ½ teaspoon pepper. Bring to a boil, lower heat at once, and simmer for 2 hours, stirring occasionally. Discard the bay leaf. Stir 2 cups dry red wine into the sauce. Add about 1½ to 2 pounds fish (halibut or rockfish) and ½ pound each raw shrimp and scallops. Cover and simmer for 10 minutes.

Add ½ pound crabmeat, then place a dozen clams on top of the sauce. Cover and simmer 5 minutes longer, or until the clamshells open and the fish flakes easily.

Serve immediately in wide soup bowls with chopped parsley or snipped wild chives sprinkled over each serving. Garlic French bread goes well with this.

HALIBUT QUICHE

Is there any end to the different ways to prepare halibut? Such a huge fish should have numerous recipes dedicated to it.

Prepare pastry for a 9-inch single-crust pie and line a pie plate with it. Place 1 cup flaked, precooked halibut in the prepared pie crust. Shred 1 cup Swiss cheese and chop ½ cup onion, then sprinkle these over the halibut. Beat 4 eggs lightly and beat in 1 cup half-and-half and 1 cup milk, ¾ teaspoon salt, and ¼ teaspoon pepper. Pour the egg mixture over the ingredients in the pie plate.

Bake in a 425°F. oven for 15 minutes. Reduce the oven temperature to 300°F. and continue baking for 30 minutes, or until a knife inserted comes out clean. Remove from the oven and let stand 10 minutes before cutting.   *– The Sadusky Sisters*

BAKED HALIBUT WITH SHRIMP SAUCE

Halibut is a white-fleshed fish and a favorite of many people. The flavor is quite bland, so it needs something like this Shrimp Sauce to sharpen it.

Choose a cross-cut of halibut that weighs about 4 or 5 pounds. Rinse the fish in cold water and pat dry with paper towels. Rub inside and out with a mixture of herbs such as thyme, dill, basil, chives, and tarragon. If you feel that the fish is too lean, sprinkle it frequently during baking with butter or margarine, melted in an equal amount of hot water. Bake the fish at 400°F. for 30 to 45 minutes. Test for flakiness with a fork. When it is done, carefully remove any skin and place the halibut on a heated platter.

While the fish is baking prepare the sauce. Use the basic White Sauce recipe (p. 91) and add to it a little tomato paste and herbs of your choice. Melt ¼ to ½ pound Cheddar or Cheshire cheese in a double boiler with 1 tablespoon margarine and ½ teaspoon dry

mustard. You might also like to add a few grains of cayenne pepper. Stir the cheese mixture into the white sauce carefully, then stir in a cup of tiny Petersburg shrimp. Sprinkle lemon juice liberally over the halibut, then pour the sauce over it. Decorate with slices of stuffed olives.

NANCY'S HALIBUT CHOWDER

A fish chowder like this is so rich it is practically a meal in itself. This is terrific served with Bread Sticks (p. 83) or Sourdough Rolls (p. 84).

Melt ¼ cup butter or margarine in a soup kettle. Blend in ¼ cup flour and 1 teaspoon sea salt. Add 3½ cups fish stock. If you don't have quite that much stock, add water to make up the difference. Blend the stock in gradually and cook slowly until thick and smooth, stirring constantly. Add to the stock as much previously cooked halibut as you want. Feel free to add a few potatoes, cubed and cooked, at this point, too. Continue simmering for 10 or 15 minutes. Add ½ to 1 cup cream. (The amount depends on how rich you like your chowder.) Ladle the chowder into serving bowls and garnish with a sprinkle of finely chopped parsley.   *– Nancy Sadusky*

STUFFED FISH ROLLS

These rolls make a tremendous main dish for a seafood dinner. Serve them along with Clam Chowder (p. 22), Layered Shrimp Salad (p. 29), and Baked Salmon (p. 14), and you will be serving a meal to remember.

Place 6 halibut fillets on a flat surface. Combine 1½ cups soft bread crumbs, ¾ cup whole wheat cracker crumbs, 3 tablespoons chopped fresh parsley (or the equivalent in dried parsley flakes), 4 tablespoons melted butter or margarine, and 1½ tablespoons dry sherry. Toss gently. Spoon equal portions of this filling on each fillet and spread evenly but not quite to the edges. Roll up each fillet and fasten with a skewer or toothpick. Put 4 tablespoons margarine and 2 tablespoons dry sherry in a shallow baking dish and place in a preheated 400°F. oven. Then place the fish rolls in the baking dish and baste with the butter-sherry sauce. Bake for 15 minutes, turning once with tongs. (If the rolls are too difficult to turn, skip this last step.)

STUFFED HALIBUT FILLETS

Béchamel sauce sounds fancy, but it is nothing more than a jazzed-up White Sauce (see p. 91). Instead of using just milk for the liquid, béchamel calls for chicken stock and cream and your choice of seasonings such as onion, bay leaf, thyme, and so on.

Spread large, thin halibut fillets with the following mixture: dry bread crumbs, lemon juice, salt, pepper, minced dried chives, a dash of cayenne pepper, and ½ teaspoon each of chervil, curry powder, dill seed, and thyme. Add enough melted margarine to give the mixture a spreadable consistency. Roll up the fillets and skewer closed with a toothpick.

Arrange a layer of soda crackers in the bottom of a baking dish. Brush the rolled fillets with melted margarine and place on top of the crackers. These crackers keep the fish from sticking to the baking dish and should be discarded after use.

Bake in a preheated 350°F. oven

until the fish flakes when tested with a fork. Serve with béchamel sauce. You might want to add capers or chopped gherkins to the sauce.

CAMPFIRE BROILED SALMON

For this recipe you'll need a good hot campfire and not just a smoking deal. Drive two stout pronged branches into the ground on either side of the fire and have a few slender green sticks ready.

Fillet a good-sized dressed salmon, leaving the skin on. Make 2 long fillets or several shorter ones. Thread the fillets on the green sticks and season them well to taste. Be sure that the prongs in the upright sticks are from 20 to 24 inches above the bed of coals. Lay a stick with its threaded fillets across the prongs of the upright sticks, placing the skin side of the salmon down.

After the salmon begins to cook, baste frequently with melted butter or margarine or other sauce. Broil until the fish is well done and flakes easily. Just before it seems to be done turn the fillets skin-side up for about 5 minutes, then back again for the final basting. Try serving shoestring potatoes and onion rings with this.

SEAFOOD SALAD

If you don't have salmon, you can use rockfish, sea bass, or even canned tuna in this recipe, but we prefer cooked salmon.

Thinly slice ½ cup each of celery and green onion (tops and all), and tear about 1 cup lettuce into bite-size pieces. Drain and chop ¼ cup pimientos and ½ cup clams. Peel ½ cup shrimp. Melt 1 tablespoon butter or margarine in a frying pan and sauté the shrimp and clams for 3 or 4 minutes, stirring as they cook.

Mix together ½ cup mayonnaise, ½ cup dairy sour cream, and a few squirts from the homestead lemon (one of those plastic lemon juice containers that looks like a lemon). Beat until smooth. Add the clams, shrimp, fish, 1 cup cooked vegetables, and other seasonings to taste. (Sea salt, pepper, thyme, marjoram, and a dash of cayenne are all good.) Toss carefully and refrigerate for at least 2 hours. When serving, garnish with wedges of hard-cooked egg.

BAKED SALMON

King (Chinook) or red (sockeye) salmon have become our favorites of all the salmon. Both are wonderful cooked in many ways. Salmon can be dried, smoked, frozen, and canned. Maybe the reason we like kings and reds so well is that they are richer than other salmon. Every calorie is worth it, though, especially when served with the classic egg sauce.

Choose a hefty chunk of king salmon or a whole red one to bake. (There are many ways to use leftover salmon, so don't be afraid to bake a large piece.) Rinse and pat the fish dry with paper towels. Rub it inside and out with your choice of herbs mixed with salt and pepper. Slice an onion or two and lay the slices within the body cavity. Put the salmon on a piece of heavy-duty foil about 3 times the size of the fish and place in a roasting pan. Fold the foil loosely over the salmon but crimp the foil to make it airtight. Bake the salmon in a preheated 375°F. oven for 30 minutes.

Fold back the foil to expose the fish completely and bake until it flakes easily with a fork. Don't bake it too long, because it can easily become over-dry. Carefully lift the salmon to a heated platter. Peel off the skin if it comes easily and lift out the backbone. Serve with fluffy mashed potatoes and green peas grown in your own Alaskan garden.

EGG SAUCE

Using 2 hard-cooked eggs per person, prepare the egg sauce by following the basic White Sauce recipe (p. 91), then chopping and adding the eggs and any seasonings you wish. Make plenty of sauce; you'll need it for the leftover salmon.

SALMON LOAF

Salmon loaf is a bonus made from left-over baked salmon and it is always much appreciated — maybe even more so than the original dish.

Remove crusts from a couple of slices of bread. Pull the soft part of the slices into small pieces and put into a bowl. Pour a small amount of milk over the bread crumbs and allow to stand for a few minutes, until the bread is soaked. Flake the salmon into the bowl. If you have any leftover rice or mashed potatoes, add a little of one or the other. (Sometimes we even use a few spoonfuls of Potato Buds.) Season to taste. You will want to add some chopped onion (chives or green onions will do), thyme, marjoram, cayenne, vegetable seasoning, chopped bell pepper pieces, and whatever else strikes your fancy. Then break an egg into the mixture and stir it in well. Grease a loaf pan thoroughly and pack your salmon into it. Melt 2 tablespoons margarine and drizzle it over the top. Bake in a preheated 350°F. oven for 45 minutes to 1 hour, depending on how thick the loaf is. Serve with reheated egg sauce. Salmon loaf is good served cold, too, and it makes excellent sandwiches.

SALMON CAKES

Maybe you don't have quite enough salmon left for a salmon loaf, but you do have plenty of mashed potatoes and egg sauce remaining. Here is what you should do with them.

Put your mashed potatoes in a bowl and add the flaked salmon. Crack in an egg and stir the whole lot to blend well. Put in any additional seasonings you like and add a little whole wheat flour, so that the mixture is not soupy but rather stiff.

Melt some butter or margarine over medium heat in a heavy frying pan. Drop the stiff batter by heaping spoonfuls into the pan. Meanwhile, reheat the leftover egg sauce. When the cakes begin to brown on the bottom, turn them over carefully and brown on the other side. Remove cakes to a heated platter and serve with the egg gravy.

SALMON SANDWICHES

Another good use for leftover salmon and egg gravy. These sandwiches make a great addition to a tailgate picnic.

Spread a little butter or margarine on the sandwich bread. This will help to keep the egg sauce from softening the bread too much. Flake the salmon into a small bowl and add just a little egg gravy (or mayonnaise) and your choice of seasonings. (We like onion powder, salt, and pepper.) Blend care-

fully. Spread both pieces of bread lightly with the egg sauce and then spread the fish mixture on one slice. Close the sandwich and cut it in half diagonally.

If you don't intend for the sandwich to be eaten immediately, wrap it in plastic wrap and then in aluminum foil.

SALMON CROQUETTES

This recipe couldn't be much simpler to make. Serve the croquettes with leftover egg sauce.

Flake the leftover salmon and add about one-quarter as much cold cooked rice. Stir gently to blend. Put in a few drops of lemon juice and onion juice. If onion juice isn't available, sprinkle in a few dehydrated minced onions. Shape into 1½-inch balls or into rolls that are roughly 1 inch in diameter by 2 inches long. Coat with fine dry bread crumbs. Fry in deep fat at about 375°F. Don't fry too many at one time. Remove the croquettes from the fat when they are well crusted and brown; drain them on paper towels.

GRILLED SALMON

Try this recipe sometime with red snapper or sea bass. You can also crumble a little feta cheese into the mixture if you want to make it a bit different. You'll need 4 salmon steaks or fillets.

Get the charcoal fire going and allow it to burn down to ashy gray coals. Place the grill about 6 inches above the coals. Combine the following in a bowl: salt and black pepper to taste; 1 green pepper, seeded, membrane removed, and cut into thin strips; 12 pitted black olives; ½ cup finely chopped sweet onion; 1 teaspoon

finely chopped garlic; 1½ cups chopped tomato; ¼ teaspoon dried oregano; ¼ teaspoon dried red pepper flakes; and 1 bay leaf, finely crumbled. Stir briefly to mingle the flavors.

Place a 12-inch strip of heavy-duty aluminum foil on a flat surface. Lay 1 salmon steak in the center of the foil. Put 1 teaspoon olive oil and one-quarter of the mixture on the steak. Repeat with the remaining steaks. Fold the long sides of the foil over the fish to make an airtight fold along the entire length of the foil. Fold up the ends of the foil, leaving some space inside to allow for expansion. Place the 4 foil packets on the grill and cook for about 15 to 18 minutes, depending upon the thickness of the steaks. When done, place the packets on serving plates and open the foil carefully to allow steam to escape.

SALMON SALAD

There are many different kinds of salmon salad; they range from simple ones like this to elaborate concoctions.

Mix lightly 3 cups of small salmon chunks (smoked salmon is ideal for this), and 1 cup chopped celery with a few celery leaves chopped in. Add 3 hard-cooked eggs, diced, half a dozen sweet pickles, sliced, salt and pepper to taste, a dash of lemon juice, and just enough mayonnaise to bind ev-

erything together. Chill before serving and garnish with cucumber and tomato slices. This salad is especially good served with fresh Sourdough French Bread (p. 85).

SOFT-SMOKED SALMON

This soft-smoked salmon is delicious and simple to make, but you must follow the directions closely — it's especially important not to leave the fish in the salt mixture too long.

Fillet an average-size (5- to 7-pound) red or silver salmon. Cut the fillets diagonally in the direction the ribs lay, into approximately 1-inch-wide pieces. Separate the thinner from the thicker pieces.

Coat the pieces with Morton's Sugar Cure. (This is a mixture that is mainly salt with a little brown sugar and some spices thrown in.) Do *not* add water to the cure to make a brine — just coat the fish in the Sugar Cure. Leave the cure on the thinner pieces for just 30 minutes, then rinse it off *completely* and pat the pieces dry with paper towels. Leave the cure on the thicker pieces for 1 hour, then rinse and pat dry as you did the thinner pieces.

Arrange the pieces on the rack from the smoker and dry them with a fan until a glaze forms (this usually takes between 1 and 2 hours).

About 15 minutes before the fish is ready to go in the smoker, take the smoker outdoors and plug it in to begin warming up. (I use a Little Chief electric smoker.) When the fish is ready, put it in the warm smoker, with the thinner pieces on the top shelves and the thicker ones below. Fill the chip pan with hickory chips. I try to keep the internal temperature of the smoker between 110°F. and 160°F. for best results. The outside temperature will influence the temperature inside the smoker, of course.

Refill the chip pan every 90 minutes or so. The fish will be ready to eat in about 5 hours — it will have a hard, shiny coat on the outside and will be flaky inside. It is delicious right out of the smoker. To store this soft-smoked salmon, wrap it in aluminum foil (*not* plastic wrap) and keep it in the refrigerator. It's best if eaten within 2 weeks, but it will keep up to a month.

– *John Sadusky*

SALMON BALLS

Canned salmon is fine for these delectable salmon balls, though freshly caught and cooked salmon tastes even better.

Let one 8-ounce package cream cheese stand at room temperature until soft. Drain and clean as needed a 1-pound can of salmon. Combine the cream cheese, salmon, 2 teaspoons lemon juice, 3 teaspoons grated onion, 1 teaspoon prepared horseradish, ¼ teaspoon liquid smoke, and ¼ teaspoon salt. Mix carefully to a smooth consistency and form into balls. Roll the balls in finely chopped nuts, either pecans or walnuts, or roll in chopped olives. Refrigerate for several hours before serving. These balls can be successfully frozen.

– *Lois Armstrong*

GRAYLING FRY

As you have probably noticed, fish does not stay fresh for very long. Grayling is the hardest to keep and really should be used the same day it is caught. It is great cooked right in camp after catching.

Roll pan-sized grayling in flour or fine cracker crumbs. Fry in light olive oil over medium-high heat in a heavy skillet. Turn the grayling carefully with spatulas so that the delicate fish does not fall apart. After 10 minutes it should be browned on both sides; test with a fork to see if it will flake easily. Sprinkle with a little salt, pepper, and thyme. Grayling has a slight thyme-like scent of its own, and using that herb enhances the scent.

HOOLIGAN FRY

Hooligan is just the corrupted form of eulachon, the name of a small smeltlike fish that runs in great numbers in some of our rivers each spring. Also called candlefish, these fish are extremely oily and must be cooked just right or the oil will make them unpalatable. Be sure to prepare plenty of these, since people will no doubt eat more than you expect.

Use either freshly dressed or completely thawed frozen hooligan. Wipe dry. Coat the bottom of a heavy frying pan with vegetable oil. Place the pan over medium heat and heat the oil to almost smoking hot. While the pan is heating, the fish should be dipped in slightly beaten egg, then in cracker crumbs, dry bread crumbs, flour, or cornmeal (any combination will do). Prepare enough fish for one panful at a time. Put them on to fry and cook quickly. (You may need to raise the heat.) Speedy cooking prevents the little fish from becoming soft and ensures a good crisp crust. When the fish are put on to fry, set the oven to 350°F. and place a good-sized baking pan inside. The oven should be hot by the time the first panful of fish is fried. The hooligan may then be placed in the pan and kept hot. This step in the preparation should not be omitted because it also helps to dry the fish somewhat and gets rid of their excess fat. Hooligan are so fatty that if fried and served without this "drying off" they will be too oily for most people to enjoy.

Fry as many fish as you wish and transfer each successive panful to the baking pan in the oven. Between each frying, pour excess fat out of the frying pan. Leave the fish in the oven for 15 minutes after putting the last ones in. Serve on a large platter surrounded by lemon wedges and sprigs of parsley. Hot rolls and cole slaw should accompany fried hooligan.

NANCY'S FISH STOCK

It's a good idea to have fish stock on hand to use in soups, chowders, and other fish dishes. It can be made in various ways, and any kind of fish can be used to make a fine stock.

Throw the bones and head of a halibut in a kettle of water. Simmer with chopped celery, parsley, and onions; season with sea salt, pepper, and any other spices and herbs you prefer. Allow the stock to simmer for an hour or more — at least until the flesh falls off the head. Remove the pot from the heat and allow to cool. When the

18

broth is cool, strain into freezer containers and discard all but the stock.

– Nancy Sadusky

TO VARY: Some cooks like to add 2 or 3 cups of dry white wine to the above stock when it is about halfway through its cooking time.

FLAKED FISH HASH

If you need a different dish to serve for breakfast and you have some leftover salmon or halibut, this is just the thing.

Dice several strips of bacon and pan-fry until crisp. Meanwhile mix together 2 cups grated or chopped cold boiled potatoes, 1 tablespoon minced chives or onions, sea salt, and pepper. When the bacon bits are fried add them to the potato mixture, together with 2 cups flaked fish. Stir just enough to blend well. Place the mixture in the hot bacon drippings and fry until brown. Do *not* stir. Fold over and serve as you would an omelet.

FISH AND TOMATO SOUP

If you like the flavor of tomatoes with fish you should like this. It is a whiz! After the soup is poured into serving bowls sprinkle the top of each serving with finely snipped wild chives.

Fry 4 slices of bacon until crisp; drain and crumble. Combine bacon with 2 or 3 tablespoons minced wild chives or green onions and ½ cup minced celery leaves (with a bit of celery stalk). Add 2 cups of Nancy's Fish Stock (p. 18) and simmer for 15 minutes. Add sea salt, pepper, oregano, and other seasonings of your choice, and stir in ¼ cup uncooked rice. Simmer for 15 minutes longer. Add 2 cups tomato juice and 2 cups cubed or flaked fish — any lean white-meated variety will do. Simmer again until the fish and rice are tender. Just before serving, drop a small dollop of butter or margarine into each bowl.

TOMATO POACHED FISH

Put a rack in the bottom of your largest saucepan. Then cut cheesecloth or similar loosely woven cloth to make a bag for the fish. The bag ensures that the fish does not fall apart as it cooks.

Cut lean, white-meated fish into serving-size portions and place inside the square of cloth. Secure the cloth around the fish so that it will remain inside the improvised bag. Place the bag of fish into the saucepan and add enough fish stock to almost cover it. Add a little tomato paste (from the tube) or half a small can of tomato juice. Bring to a boil and reduce the heat immediately to low; simmer until the fish can be pierced easily with a fork. Remove the bag of fish and thicken the stock slightly with a little flour to make a sauce. Carefully remove the fish from the cloth and place on a serving platter. Garnish with lemon twists and sprigs of parsley. Pass the sauce separately.

OVEN-FRIED FISH FILLETS

You can use almost any kind of good fish for this — rockfish, trout, and salmon are all outstanding. This is a real "hurry up" dish, which we all need at times.

Preheat the oven to 500°F. while preparing the fish. Cut about 2 pounds of fillets into serving-size pieces. Combine 1 tablespoon sea salt with 1 cup

of milk. Dip the fish pieces in the milk and then dredge well with fine dry bread crumbs. Place in a well-greased shallow baking pan. Pour melted margarine or olive oil over the fish. Place the pan near the top of your hot oven and bake for 10 to 12 minutes. The fish should flake easily when done. Don't bake too long!

SALMON PATTIES WITH SPINACH SAUCE

You might call this an unusual combination. You might also call it a good one. If you use frozen spinach, thaw it completely and then pat it dry.

Drain a 1-pound can of salmon and remove the bones and skin. Mix the salmon with ½ cup dry bread crumbs, ½ cup chopped spinach, 1 egg, ½ cup grated onion, and ⅛ teaspoon cayenne pepper. Form into patties and fry in a hot skillet.

To make the sauce, melt 2 tablespoons butter in a saucepan, then blend in 2 tablespoons flour. Stir in 1½ cups milk, 2 ounces Swiss cheese, ½ teaspoon Dijon mustard, ¼ teaspoon pepper, and ¼ teaspoon salt. Heat slowly until the mixture thickens. Add 1 cup chopped spinach. Remove the patties to a serving tray, pour the sauce over them, and serve.

– Bekki Chapek

COME OUT OF YOUR SHELL:
Clams, Scallops, Shrimp, and Crabs

There are numerous species of shellfish in Alaska, but we have included in this chapter only the ones we most enjoy.

With respect to clams — be sure to harvest them only from approved beaches or used canned ones. This is to avoid PSP (paralytic shellfish poisoning), which is no joke. Always discard the dark portions of the clams.

UNCLE JOE'S OLD-FASHIONED CLAMBAKE

Not much cleaning up or dishwashing needs to be done after eating these clams. No utensils are needed, either, unless you are serving corn on the cob, and then only knives for the butter. A pile of paper napkins will come in handy, and people can snatch them as needed. Two or 3 paper plates scattered around the table to receive the discarded clamshells and the uneaten necks, and that's it!

First, dig a pit in the beach at least a foot deep (deeper if possible). Line it with fairly large rocks, with a layer of smaller stones on top of them. Build a fire on top of the stones and keep it well stoked with wood until it is really roaring. Then allow it to die down. This process should take an hour or more.

In the meantime, scrub the clams well in seawater, allowing about a quart of clams for each hungry person. Our clambakes always included corn on the cob. If you want to try that, you will need corn that is still in its husks. Dip the corn in seawater, too. Put the washed clams in a large burlap bag and tie the ends with wire. Rake the ashes off the rocks, working quickly, so the white-hot stones don't get a chance to cool. Then place the bag on the hot rocks and pile the corn around it. Cover the lot with seaweed or with several layers of canvas weighted down around the edges. Steam for an hour or more.

When the clams are ready to eat, place the burlap bag in the center of the picnic table and slit it open so that people can help themselves. If you think seasonings are needed, place the usual assortment on the table, but you will probably find that the clams disappear without their benefit. Put a dish of butter or margarine on the table, too, for the corn.

21

STEAMED CLAMS

The traditional way to eat steamed clams is to dip them first in their nectar and then in melted butter.

Scrub the clams — about a quart per person to be served — and place them in a deep kettle. Change the water several times while scrubbing to make sure that all sand is eliminated. Add a couple of tablespoons of water for each quart of clams and cover the kettle tightly. Steam over low heat for about 15 minutes, or until the shells open slightly. (Discard any that don't open.) With a slotted spoon remove the clams to large soup dishes.

Small bowls, half filled with very hot water and then filled to near the top with melted butter, should accompany each serving. The melted butter will remain floating on top of the water. Add a few drops of lemon juice and a sprig of parsley to each bowl, if you wish. Lift the clams from their shells by their black necks and dip them in the butter, eating all but the necks. Serve the liquid left in the kettle in small glasses. This clam nectar is delicious.

FRIED CLAMS

Be sure to cut the dark portion of the clams away before cooking. It doesn't pay to take chances: remember PSP.

Scrub the shells of the clams and steam them for a few minutes — just long enough for the shells to open. With a sharp knife, cut the muscles and remove the clams from their shells. Season the clams to taste and dredge with flour (try using whole wheat flour sometime). Heat deep fat to 375°F. and fry the clams just until browned, turning once. Drain on a double thickness of paper towels. The clams can also be fried in bacon fat in a heavy skillet.

CLAM MILK STEW

For eye appeal, sprinkle a few snips of wild chives or parsley on top of each serving. Paprika is also attractive.

Using ground fresh clams or canned minced clams, make a milk stew by heating clam juice, margarine, and milk to just under the boiling point. Add the clams and simmer for 10 minutes, seasoning to taste. Onion powder or minced onion is sometimes used in milk stew, but keep the ingredients simple. Adjust proportions to your liking.

CLAM CHOWDER

To make Manhattan clam chowder use the recipe below, but substitute water for the milk and cream. You may wish to experiment with a little milk in place of some of the water, but Manhattan clam chowder always requires tomatoes, and tomatoes and milk together must be handled with care to avoid curdling. Most recipes for Manhattan clam chowder call for canned tomatoes, but I just use a little purée.

Grind clams or use canned minced clams, 6 to 8 ounces per person. Heat the clams and clam liquid to boiling. Add pepper, thyme, marjoram, crushed red pepper flakes, and minced onion flakes or their equivalent in fresh onion (you may not need to add salt). Parsley or chervil flakes or snipped fresh chives help the appearance of the chowder. Add part half-and-half and part milk — enough for each serving. When the chowder is hot again, but not boiling,

add bacon bits or diced frizzled salt pork to taste. Last of all, stir in some Potato Buds until the chowder thickens a little. Remove from the heat. Taste for seasoning and correct it if you like. If the chowder seems too thick add a bit more milk. Serve with Herbed French Bread (p. 87) or oyster crackers.

CLAM FRITTERS

Instead of ordinary cooking oil try using a good grade of olive oil for pan-frying occasionally.

Grind fresh clams or use canned minced clams to the amount of 1 cup. Drain and measure the juice; add enough milk to make ⅓ cup liquid. In a mixing bowl beat one egg, then add the liquid. Sift together ⅔ cup flour, 1 teaspoon baking powder, ½ teaspoon salt, a liberal dash of black pepper, and any other seasonings you wish. Add this to the liquids and blend; then add the clams. Heat a heavy frying pan and pour in a liberal amount of vegetable oil (or use bacon fat if available). When the oil is really hot, drop the batter by generous spoonfuls into the pan. Fry until browned on each side. You can also fry these fritters in deep fat heated to 375°F. For cocktail-size fritters, use a much smaller spoon for dropping the batter into the fat.

SCALLOPED CLAMS

Clams are extremely versatile and lend themselves to all sorts of dishes. We think this is one of the best.

Butter a large casserole and arrange 2½ to 3½ cups finely chopped or ground clams in alternating layers with 1 to 1¼ cups cracker crumbs.

Melt 2 tablespoons butter or margarine in a skillet and stir in the same amount of flour. Gradually add 1½ cups milk, stirring diligently as it cooks. Add a dash of cayenne and ½ teaspoon each of thyme, marjoram, and red pepper flakes. A little sea salt should be added, too, but go cautiously here and taste the sauce before you put in too much. Pour this thickened sauce over the clams in the casserole.

Melt a tablespoon or more of margarine and stir into it dry bread or cracker crumbs. Scatter the buttered crumbs on top of the casserole and sprinkle lightly with paprika. Bake in a preheated 375°F. oven for 30 minutes, or until well browned.

SKILLET HASH

This hash can be cooked on top of the stove or in the oven, but it is a bit more convenient to do it on the stove. In any case, be sure to press the mixture down after turning it. Otherwise it won't brown properly.

In a skillet fry 4 pieces of bacon until crisp. Drain on paper towels and then crumble. Add 4 tablespoons butter or margarine to the skillet and stir in 1 cup chopped onion. Sauté until the onion is translucent. Add 2 cups of peeled, diced potatoes that have been cooked in their jackets, and 1 cup or more of drained minced clams. Add chopped parsley, sea salt, and pepper to taste. Press down with a spatula or pancake turner. Cook over medium-high heat until the bottom is browned. Turn with the spatula, mixing some of the brown crust into the hash as you turn it. Press down again, and again cook until the bottom is brown. Top with grated Parmesan cheese and the crumbled bacon. Cov-

er the skillet tightly and cook for about 1 or 2 minutes more, just until the cheese melts. Garnish with parsley and serve at once.

CLAM GULCH CLAMBURGERS

You don't know what you have missed if you haven't tried clamburgers. You can use either clams that have been freshly dug and prepared or canned ones — either way you won't be sorry. Just be sure to mince them finely.

Drain the minced clams well. Add a slightly beaten egg, salt, pepper, onion juice (or minced chives), and ½ cup cornmeal. Be careful not to get the mixture too juicy or it won't hold its shape. Heat a heavy frying pan to sizzling hot and add enough bacon drippings or cooking oil to coat the bottom of the pan. Drop the clam batter by tablespoonfuls into the hot pan; do not drop the patties too close together.

When a burger begins to bubble and sizzle, flip it over gently so as not to break it. Sauté until brown on the other side, then transfer quickly to buttered toast and cover with another piece of toast. You might add a few drops of lemon juice or a sprinkling of catsup to these.

STUFFED CLAMS

These are actually clamshells stuffed with clam filling, and they make for really good eating.

Combine in a bowl 1½ cups soft bread crumbs, 8 ounces canned minced clams (well drained), ¼ cup grated cheese, 1 tablespoon parsley flakes, ¼ teaspoon garlic powder, ¼

teaspoon sea salt, 2 tablespoons olive oil, and 1 teaspoon lemon juice. Toss lightly to mix and stuff 8 to 10 scrubbed clamshells with this mixture. Foil muffin cups may be used if no clamshells are at hand. Place the shells on a cookie sheet and bake in a preheated 375°F. oven for 15 minutes, or until the filling is hot and golden. Serve with buttered toast fingers.

SHEPHERD'S CLAM PIE

There is no reason why shepherd's pie has to be made with red meat, so we decided to try it with clams. This is a good recipe if you are looking for some way to use up leftover mashed potatoes.

If no leftover mashed potatoes are on hand, it will be necessary to make up some for this recipe. Prepare as you would for any meal, with milk, butter or margarine, salt and pepper, and perhaps some finely snipped chives.

Melt ¼ cup butter or margarine in a heavy frying pan. Add 1 cup chopped onions and ¾ cup chopped celery (or less). Cook until the onions are translucent. Add about 3 cups of minced clams (reserve the liquid). Add enough water to the clam liquid to make 2 cups total and add to the clams in the frying pan. Stir in ¼ cup flour and cook the mixture until thick. Now add ½ cup carrots, thinly sliced, and ½ cup green peas, fresh or frozen. Season with sea salt, black pepper, a dash of cayenne, and any other seasonings you like.

Butter a 1½-quart casserole dish and pour in the clam mixture. Spread the mashed potatoes evenly over the top. Sprinkle with chopped parsley or paprika. Bake at 425°F. for 20 to 30 minutes.

CLAM PAN ROAST

Here's your chance to experiment with herbs and other seasonings.

Scrub enough clams to yield about a pint after they are steamed and shucked. Steam them until they open, then drain and shuck, reserving the liquid. Mix together 1¼ cups fine dry bread crumbs with ½ cup melted butter. Put a thin layer of the mixture in a shallow buttered baking dish. Cover the layer with half the clams. Sprinkle with salt, pepper, cayenne, chervil, marjoram, onion powder, and any other seasonings you like. Add 2 tablespoons clam juice and 1 tablespoon milk or cream. Repeat the whole process with the remaining buttered crumbs and clams. Cover the top with a layer of dry crumbs. Bake at 450°F. for 30 minutes. This recipe will serve 3 or 4 people.

CLAM SOUFFLÉ

Who would have thought you could make an acceptable soufflé from clams? You can, if you use a little care.

In a small bowl stir together ½ cup mayonnaise, 4 tablespoons flour, ¼ teaspoon sea salt, and a dash of pepper. Slowly add 4 tablespoons milk, then 1½ cups finely minced drained clams, 1½ teaspoons lemon juice, and 1 teaspoon grated onion. Beat 4 room-temperature egg whites until stiff peaks form. Very gently fold the egg whites into the mayonnaise mixture. Spoon into a greased baking dish, making sure that there is room for the soufflé to rise. Place the baking dish in a pan of hot water before setting it in a preheated 325°F. oven. Bake for 30 to 40 minutes, or until the soufflé is delicately brown on top.

EXOTIC STEAMED CLAMS

We don't make this recipe for steamed clams very often, but it does make a refreshing change from the humdrum homestead fare.

In a heavy skillet, pan-fry 1 large onion, finely chopped, in ¼ cup oil until soft. Add 1 clove garlic, finely minced, and a 1-inch piece of ginger root, also finely minced. Seed and cut into thin rings 2 hot fresh green chili peppers and add these to the skillet. Stir in 2 teaspoons ground cumin, ½ teaspoon turmeric, ½ teaspoon sea salt, and ⅓ cup water. Sauté all this for 2 more minutes. Add 2 cups loosely packed grated coconut and 1 more cup of water. Cook for 2 more minutes. Now add 24 steamer clams, cover the skillet tightly, and steam for 5 minutes, or just until the clamshells open. Serve at once.

SEAFOOD CHOWDER

If you like "chowdery" soups, here is one that is quite different from the usual clam or fish chowder.

Melt 4 tablespoons butter or margarine in a large soup pot. Add 1 cup finely chopped onion and 1 cup diced celery and cook, stirring constantly, until the vegetables are translucent. Add 2½ cups diced raw potatoes and 3 cups water and cook until the potatoes are tender. Add 1 cup flaked crab meat and 1 cup shelled shrimp. (Freshly cleaned and cooked seafood is best but canned seafood is acceptable.) Simmer gently for 5 minutes, or until the seafood is heated through. Now add about 1¼ teaspoons sea salt, a couple of dashes black pepper, a smidgen of cayenne, 1 quart fresh milk, and 1 cup grated American

cheese. Heat again, very slowly, just until the cheese melts. Serve in large soup bowls. Sprinkle chopped parsley or chives and tiny pieces of pimiento over the surface of each serving. Try croutons with this hearty chowder.

To make the croutons, simply butter slices of bread, sprinkle with ground thyme (and other herbs, if you wish), and cut the bread into small cubes. Arrange the cubes on a cookie sheet and bake in a hot oven for about 10 minutes. They can be either hot or cold when served. The best croutons are made from stale bread, and either white or whole wheat bread may be used.

CRAB COCKTAIL

Here is a good beginning for an all-seafood dinner. Finish it off with Baked Salmon (p. 14) or Beer Batter Halibut (p. 11), and it will be a meal to remember.

Prepare cocktail sauce by combining ⅔ cup catsup, ⅓ cup chili sauce, 2 teaspoons horseradish, a couple of good squirts from the homestead lemon, 3 teaspoons finely snipped wild chives, a dash of cayenne, a few drops of Tabasco sauce, ¼ cup finely chopped celery, and ½ cup white wine. Stir just enough to mingle all the ingredients well. Chill. Spoon a teaspoonful of the sauce into the bottom of some cocktail glasses. Add flaked crab meat, small avocado cubes, and grapefruit sections in equal parts. Finish off with more sauce and have extra sauce available on the table for those who may care for it.

KING CRAB AND GREEN STUFF

If you don't have king crabs on hand use dungeness or snow crabs. The only problem is finding greens that are young and tender enough to use.

In a shallow casserole place a generous layer of cooked chopped greens. All should be young and tender and it is better to have more than one species. How about dandelion, nettles, fireweed shoots, chickweed, or other native greens? Or, if you prefer, use garden spinach or chard. Next arrange a thick layer of flaked crab meat, freshly cooked or canned and drained. Pour cheese sauce over the crab and sprinkle with buttered crumbs. Put under the broiler for about 5 minutes. Serve immediately.

To make the cheese sauce all you need do is make a thick White Sauce (p. 91), add enough grated mild cheese to suit your taste, and allow it to melt. Also stir in any other seasonings you wish, such as onion juice, minced chives, or whatever.

ALASKA DEVILED CRAB

King crab is the best kind of crab to use in this dish, but the other species will do if king is not available.

Preheat the oven to 400°F. In the top of a double boiler, melt ¼ cup margarine. Stir in 2 tablespoons flour, 1 tablespoon minced chervil (fresh or dried), 2 teaspoons lemon juice, 1 teaspoon prepared mustard, ½ teaspoon horseradish, and 1 teaspoon sea salt. Slowly add 1 cup of milk. Cook over boiling water, stirring until thickened. Add 2 cups cooked and shelled crab meat and 2 minced hard-cooked eggs.

Spoon into 6 individual custard cups, ramekins, or scallop shells. Combine ½ cup soft bread crumbs with 2 tablespoons melted margarine and then sprinkle over the mixture. Bake for 10 minutes, or until brown and bubbly.

CRAB IN CHEESE SAUCE

Jazz up some basic White Sauce (p. 91) by melting cheese into it in a double boiler and seasoning it to taste.

Keep the cheese sauce warm in the double boiler. Collect young dandelion greens and maybe a few tight dandelion buds. Wash thoroughly through 2 or 3 waters, lifting the greens up out of the water to shed sand and soil. Cook briefly in just the water clinging to the leaves. When cooked and drained well, chop and season the greens with sea salt, pepper, and any other seasonings you wish. Arrange a layer of the greens in a shallow baking dish. Over the greens scatter 1 cup of cooked crab meat. Pour the warm cheese sauce over all. Bake at 350°F. until well heated and lightly browned. Buttered crumbs can be spooned over the sauce before baking if you wish.

CRAB CAKES

If you have plenty of crab left over from a crab feed, this is a wonderful way to use it. Leftover salmon is good this way, too.

Beat 2 eggs slightly and add 1 cup dry bread crumbs and 3½ to 4 cups flaked crab. Stir in 2 teaspoons Worcestershire sauce, salt and pepper to taste, and 1½ to 2 teaspoons lemon juice (or several squirts from the homestead lemon).

Cook ½ cup chopped celery, 1 small onion, chopped, and half a green pepper, also chopped, in a little margarine until the onion is clear and golden (but not brown). Add to the crab mixture. Form into patties about 3 inches in diameter and refrigerate them until they are firm. Fry in a skillet until browned on both sides. Serve with toast points and a green salad.

CRAB PICNIC BUNS

Take these buns on a picnic and place them at the edge of the campfire after it dies down. They don't need to be cooked — just warm them a little for the best taste.

Cut 1 cup pitted ripe olives into fairly large pieces. Flake freshly cooked crab meat. Combine the olives, crab meat, and 1 cup diced Swiss cheese. Toss lightly to blend. Mix together ⅓ cup mayonnaise, 2 tablespoons finely minced chives or green onion, 1 tablespoon lemon juice, and salt and pepper to taste. Scoop out part of the inside of each half of some burger buns. Spread the insides with softened butter or margarine. Combine the crab meat and mayonnaise and fill the bun halves. Put the halves together and wrap each bun in heavy-duty aluminum foil. Chill in the refrigerator for at least an hour before packing in the picnic hamper.

CRAB CAKES ALASKAN

Crab cakes make a welcome change of pace in your seafood menu. Serve them with cheese sauce if you wish and with Herbed French Bread (p. 87).

Melt 2 tablespoons butter or margarine in a saucepan. Add 2 tablespoons minced fresh onion or 1 tablespoon dried minced onion and cook until the onion turns yellow. Remove from the

heat. Add 1 cup soft bread crumbs, 1 pound cooked crab meat, and salt and paprika to taste. If the mixture seems dry, add a little milk, a few drops at a time. Shape into flat cakes and sprinkle with flour. Brown quickly in margarine over medium heat. Reduce the heat and cook slowly 5 minutes longer, turning once.

CRAB LOUIS

Perhaps this is just a little brother of the real Crab Louis. It is much simpler to prepare than the real thing, though, and we think it is just as good. A lot depends on the quality of the crab you use.

Arrange shredded garden lettuce on salad plates or on one large serving plate. Heap with good-sized chunks of crab. Rub hard-cooked egg yolks through a sieve and sprinkle generously over the crab. Make a sauce by using mayonnaise as a base. Add to the mayonnaise any or all of the following in proportions to suit: finely minced green onion or chives, chili sauce, chopped sweet pickle, horseradish, lemon juice, sea salt, white pepper, chopped pimiento, and a final sprinkle of paprika. Stir to mix. If the sauce is too thick, add a few drops of vinegar or lemon juice. Put the sauce in a bowl and let each person help himself. Serve with hot garlic bread or Herbed French Bread (p. 87).

FRIED SCALLOPS

This recipe is one of the simplest and also one of the best ways for serving scallops.

Scallops should be dipped quickly in and out of cold water and dried with paper towels. Season with salt and pepper and a few grains of cayenne.

Dip in slightly beaten egg, then roll in fine dry bread crumbs.

Spread the scallops out on paper towels and let dry for about 20 minutes. Melt butter or margarine over medium heat in a large heavy skillet. Fry the scallops, stirring, for no more than 5 minutes. Be very careful not to overcook.

The scallops can also be fried in deep fat heated to 375°F. for 2 minutes. Drain the scallops on paper towels after removing them from the fat.

STIR-FRIED SCALLOPS

We prefer using the smaller bay scallops for this recipe. If you have the larger ones, cut them into 2 or 3 pieces.

Melt 2 or 3 tablespoons butter or margarine in a large frying pan. Add a pound or so of scallops. Add a tomato or two cut into several pieces, bits of green pepper, a lemon slice cut in quarters, a couple of slices from a sweet onion (or some snipped chives), and some mushrooms, sliced into rather small pieces. Add these latter ingredients in proportions to suit your taste. Stir constantly over medium heat. Very little cooking is needed, so when the peppers are soft, it is time to serve this dish.

SCALLOPS EN CASSEROLE

As most of us know, scallops are quite expensive, so a recipe like this, which uses a variety of ingredients, makes the scallops go further and is thus quite a welcome addition to our fare.

First prepare a basic White Sauce (p. 91). It would be best to double the recipe, as you will need quite a bit of sauce. To the sauce, add 6 tablespoons

dry white wine and a few finely cut slivers of crystallized ginger.

Separate the scallops and drain off any excess moisture. Sprinkle lightly with salt (sea salt is best). Set aside. Melt 2 tablespoons butter or margarine in a saucepan and cook 1½ cups thinly sliced celery, ¼ cup finely chopped onion, ½ cup fresh or frozen peas, and about ¼ pound sliced puffballs or other fresh mushrooms. You may use a can of mushrooms, drained, if no fresh ones are on hand. Cook only until tender.

Grease a 1½-quart casserole dish and in it combine the scallops, vegetables, and sauce. Sprinkle the top with bread crumbs and add a few squirts from the homestead lemon. Top with finely grated Cheddar cheese. Bake in a 350°F. oven for 20 to 30 minutes, or until bubbly and suitably browned.

SEAFOOD DINNER

Along in late August we like to have this sort of dinner, if all goes according to plan and the weatherman cooperates. We serve the seafood with garlic bread — homemade sourdough, of course — and new potatoes with new peas from the garden. The seafood served depends upon what is brought in and what is in season.

Scallops or clams should be dipped in beaten egg and then dredged with fine dry bread crumbs and fried just a couple of minutes. If the scallops are large they should be cut into halves or thirds. If you have caught some fish (small salmon steaks, for instance) it can be dredged in flour and fried until flaky. Shrimp must be beheaded, shucked, and then cooked briefly. Serve all of these things with a salad and the seasonings of your choice. We

sometimes were lucky enough to have crab with this dinner, but in recent years they seem to be scarcer.

GRILLED SCALLOPS

Scallops have become a favorite seafood on the homestead. A friend furnishes us with enough for a meal now and again, and this is one way we like to serve them.

Prepare a charcoal fire and let the coals burn down to an ashy gray. Place the grill about 6 inches above the coals. Also prepare 1 each sweet green and red bell pepper by cutting out the seeds and membranes and slicing the peppers into bite-size squares. Place the scallops on skewers alternating with the pepper squares. Refrigerate until ready to grill.

Combine in a saucepan ½ cup orange juice and ¼ cup chopped green onions (including the green part). Cook until reduced to about half the original amount. Add 2 tablespoons butter or margarine, 1 small ripe tomato, peeled and diced, and salt and pepper to taste. Keep the sauce warm while cooking the kebabs. Brush the kebabs on each side with olive oil and place them on the hot grill. Cook until done, turning now and then. Put on warm plates and pour the warm sauce over them. Garnish with chervil or parsley.

LAYERED SHRIMP SALAD

In order to really see the layers at their best, serve this salad in a clear glass salad bowl.

Tear 6 cups romaine lettuce into bite-size pieces and layer 4 cups of it in the bottom of salad bowl. Put florets from 1 pound fresh cauliflower in the next

layer. For the next three layers add snow peas, cherry tomatoes, and shrimp — in that order. Add the remaining 2 cups lettuce. Garnish by taking 6 snow peas along with hard-cooked egg and lemon slices and arranging a starburst on top.

SPICY SAUCE FOR SHRIMP SALAD

Mix together 1 cup sour cream, ¼ cup green chili or green taco sauce, 1 tablespoon grated fresh onion, 2 tablespoons sugar, 1½ teaspoons Dijon mustard, and salt to taste. Chill and serve with the layered shrimp salad.

– Barbara Sykas

GARLIC SHRIMP

This is a natural for those of you who like shrimp and garlic, too. Serve it in soup bowls with chunks of Sourdough French Bread (p. 85) for dipping into the sauce.

Dry off ¾ pound small shelled shrimp and sprinkle with coarse salt on each side. Allow to stand at room temperature for 10 minutes. In a glass or earthenware casserole, place ½ cup good olive oil, 3 large cloves garlic, coarsely chopped, and 1 dried red chili pepper, stemmed, seeded, and divided into 8 pieces. Heat in a preheated 375°F. oven until the garlic is just golden. Be careful not to overcook. Add the shrimp, toss it in the oil, and return the casserole to the oven. Cook for 5 to 10 minutes, or just until done, stirring several times during the cooking. Sprinkle in ½ teaspoon paprika, 1 tablespoon minced parsley, and perhaps a little more salt. Test by tasting before adding the salt.

SHRIMP STATESIDE STYLE

Actually a Deep South recipe, this one is also well adapted to Alaskan kitchens and has survived the journey north extremely well. But then so do most recipes, and they all have to have their beginnings somewhere. Use canned shrimp in this if it is easier.

Clean, cook, and peel 2 pounds of raw shrimp. Cook slowly 1 can (about 2½ cups) tomatoes until the liquid is almost all gone. Put in a large saucepan ¼ cup bacon drippings and 1 large onion, chopped. Cook until the onion is soft. Stir in ¼ cup flour. Add the tomatoes, 1½ cups finely sliced celery, and 2 small green bell peppers, seeded, membranes removed, and chopped fine. Cook until all the vegetables are soft. Season with 1 tablespoon Worcestershire sauce and salt to taste. Add the shrimp. Cook slowly for 20 minutes. Put in a deep baking dish. Prepare baking-powder biscuit dough from your favorite biscuit mix. Cut small biscuits and place close together over the shrimp mixture. Put any remaining biscuits on a cookie sheet and bake separately. Bake the shrimp in a preheated 450°F. oven for 15 minutes.

HOT STUFF

Hot stuff it is! You can leave out the chili powder if you wish, but we think it is the chili that gives this dish its character.

In a heavy skillet cook 3 slices of diced bacon until the fat melts. Add 3 tablespoons each chopped onion and chopped green pepper and 2 tablespoons each chopped celery and chopped parsley. Cook, stirring, until the onion is yellow. Add 1 tablespoon flour and stir until the flour browns

slightly. Add 4 cups cooked tomatoes, 1 teaspoon sea salt, a few grains cayenne pepper, and 1 teaspoon chili powder. Cook until the mixture thickens. Now add 3 cups cooked rice and 2 cups cooked shrimp, broken in pieces. Stir to mingle the flavors. Heat through and test the seasonings by tasting, adjusting if needed.

EGGS AGAIN!

Our family doesn't care too much for eggs, and it got so that whenever eggs were brought to the table somebody would chirp, "What! Eggs again!" We named this dish for that exclamation.

In a bowl beat 3 eggs until frothy and then add ½ cup diced Alaskan shrimp or crab. Add 1 cup finely chopped celery or bean sprouts and 3 or 4 thinly sliced green onions. (If no onions are handy, use snipped wild chives.) Season with sea salt, pepper, and any additional seasonings you like. Feel free to add some sliced puffballs or other edible mushrooms.

Cook this mixture by tablespoonfuls in a heavy frying pan in which olive oil or peanut oil has been heated. Add more fat as needed. To vary, you might use bits of leftover rabbit, goose, or ptarmigan in place of the shellfish.

THE BIG ONES:
Moose, Caribou, Dall Sheep, and Others

The big ones are the moose and others of that family. We also will include Dall sheep and mountain goat in this chapter, as they cannot really be called small game. Moose is probably the favorite of all our wild game. We use a prodigious amount of moose meat in one year. In our opinion, good moose meat is superior to the best beef.

What we use each year depends on what we get that season. Sometimes we find ourselves short of moose and must resort to other game or to the meat market.

We believe that the single most important thing to remember when getting the big ones is to field-dress them properly and then prepare them for the kitchen or freezer correctly.

MOOSE NOODLE SOUP

Whole wheat noodles are preferred for this, but any kind will do. The vegetables can be fresh, frozen, canned, or dried. Go easy on the salt because the soup base may well have enough for your taste. Vary quantities according to how much soup you want.

If you do not have game stock on hand, but have the bones, cook them with water to cover in a large stockpot, until what meat is left on them is so tender that it drops off the bones. Remove the bones and discard them after stripping off the meat. You should have at least 4 quarts of liquid; add water to the stock if necessary to make that amount. A couple of heaping tablespoons beef soup base will be needed (see Items to Keep on Hand, p. 94, for the name of one supplier) and any or all of the following: lima beans, black-eyed peas, pinto beans, corn, carrots, bell peppers, onions, Betty Crocker Potato Buds, dried red pepper flakes, tomato paste, dried mixed soup vegetables, black pepper, thyme, and marjoram. A bouquet garni is good, as are other herbs. Just remember that the secret to good vegetable soup is the long, slow simmering of the bones and the stock.

The whole wheat noodles are especially good with this soup and they do not need to cook too long. Read the directions on the package for their cooking time.

If you are using stock, and not

bones with meat clinging to them, you can brown some gameburger and add it to the soup.

ALASKAN SPAGHETTI

Spaghetti is a bit like chili — every cook does it differently, but every recipe seems to turn out well.

Place ½ cup olive oil and 2 tablespoons butter or margarine in a Dutch oven, together with 1 chopped green pepper, seeds and membrane removed. Add 1 onion finely chopped and a clove of garlic minced well. Fry until the onion is golden brown. Add 1½ pounds mooseburger and salt and pepper to taste. Mix to blend well and cook over medium heat, without covering but stirring now and then. Add 1 can tomatoes and 1 can tomato sauce; cover and continue cooking for about an hour.

Half an hour before the mixture is done prepare the spaghetti. Bring to a boil 2 quarts of salted water. Put in half a package of spaghetti and cook until soft. Drain in a colander and rinse with hot water under the tap. Do not omit the rinsing or the spaghetti will taste "starchy." Place the spaghetti in a large serving bowl and pour the hot meat mixture over it. Sprinkle a generous portion of grated Parmesan cheese over the top. Serve with a green salad.   *– Lois Armstrong*

PÂTÉ OF GAME LIVER (LIVER SPREAD)

Any game liver — moose, caribou, mountain sheep, wild fowl, rabbit, or others — may be used, but each may require some variation in seasonings.

This pâté can be stored in the refrigerator for several weeks and can be used in various ways.

Clean and trim the liver as needed. Simmer in slightly salted water until tender. Put through the medium blade of food chopper. Then put through the finest blade of the chopper. Let your imagination be your guide in seasoning. Dried minced chives or onions, salt, pepper, mushroom base, prepared mustard, Worcestershire sauce, catsup or pepper sauce, chopped olives, bacon bits — any or all of these would be good, as well as other herbs and spices. Combine the ground liver and seasonings with enough soft margarine or butter to moisten. Mix gently but thoroughly and pack in square plastic freezer containers. Freeze. When needed for sandwiches, thaw slightly and slice. For canapés, thaw completely and mix with mayonnaise or other salad dressing.

PEPPER STEAK

Here is a recipe that gives you an excellent use for flank steak or other potentially tough meat from wild critters.

Marinate a moose flank or other steak (see p. 92) for 3 or 4 hours. The cranberry juice mentioned as an option in the marinade recipe should be used by all means. It will enhance the steak flavor greatly. After marinating, drain the steak well and put it in a shallow baking dish with just a little water. Roast at 350°F. for an hour, covered. Remove from the oven and allow to cool enough to handle. While the steak is cooling, make the sauce.

Add a level tablespoon of beef soup base to 2 cups boiling water. Add also

33

a little soy sauce, 2 tablespoons tomato purée, dried bell pepper pieces or fresh pepper strips, 1 small onion, diced, and any seasonings you wish. Make a paste of 1 level tablespoon cornstarch and a little cold water. Stir this into the sauce and continue stirring until the sauce thickens.

When the steak has cooled enough to handle, cut it in short julienne strips and put the strips in a casserole dish. Pour the thickened sauce over the strips and bake in a 325°F. oven for 1½ hours, covered. After the first hour remove the cover and continue cooking. Serve over rice.

If you have no beef soup base, you can use game stock or bouillon cubes in the sauce recipe above.

STOCK FROM GAME

When your game is butchered there are, or certainly should be, plenty of bones which have bits of meat clinging to them. Saw the larger bones in two or crack them to expose the marrow.

Place the bones in your largest stockpot and barely cover them with cold water. Bring to a boil, then reduce the heat and simmer slowly for several hours. Let stand until cool and remove the bones. Allow the stock to become completely cold and skim off all the fat that has risen to the surface and solidified. After skimming, replace the bones in the stock and again bring to a boil. Reduce the heat to simmer. Add 1 or 2 onions peeled and diced, a couple of sliced carrots (or more), a handful of minced wild chives, a few chopped celery leaves, several peppercorns, and an herb bouquet.

Add any other seasonings you wish after taste-testing; you will want to add sea salt and perhaps some other ingredients. Cover and simmer the stock for 3 hours or more. Again test for seasoning and add anything you think it needs. Remove the herb bouquet; strain the stock and allow it to cool. Skim off any fat that may rise to the surface. Store in closed containers in the refrigerator or freezer.

This stock is not really as hard to make as it may seem. It will be the base for many future soups, gravies, sauces, and the like. It can also be used as the liquid in meat loaves, stews, and literally a hundred other dishes. Once you become accustomed to using meat stock, you will wonder how you ever cooked without it.

ROAST IN FOIL

A piece of a young black bear makes a good pot roast when it is cooked in this fashion, but we prefer moose or caribou.

In a baking pan place a large sheet of heavy-duty aluminum foil — large enough to completely wrap around the roast you will use. Place a good-sized caribou or moose roast on the foil and sprinkle 1 envelope dry onion soup mix over the meat. Spread over this the contents of 1 can cream of mushroom soup and 1 small can mushrooms (drained). Fold the foil over the roast and crimp closed, making a tight seal but a loose package for the roast. Cook in a 300°F. oven for 4 hours. The drippings may be thickened with the usual flour-and-water paste or used "as is" for gravy.

34

CARIBOU SWISS STEAK

Swiss steak is an old standby in most American homes, and rightly so. It is very good reheated the next day, too.

Pound about ¾ cup whole wheat flour into 2 pounds of 1-inch-thick caribou round or sirloin tip steak. The edge of a heavy plate or the back of a butcher knife will suffice for pounding. Fry 1 large sliced onion in 2 tablespoons hot fat in a heavy frying pan until the onion is golden. Remove from the pan and set aside. Cut the steak in serving-size pieces and put it in the frying pan. Brown well on both sides and cover with the onion slices. Add 2 teaspoons salt, 1 teaspoon dry mustard, ¼ teaspoon pepper, 1 clove garlic, finely chopped, and any other seasonings you wish. Then add ½ cup water and ½ cup canned tomatoes or tomato juice. Cover and cook on top of the stove over low heat for about 2 hours, or in the oven at a setting of 325°F.

BUBBLE AND SQUEAK

This may not be quite like the traditional Bubble and Squeak of English fame, but we think you will enjoy it anyway. This terrific one-dish meal should feed about 6 to 8 people.

Cut about 2 pounds of caribou round steak into 1-inch pieces and sauté in margarine until browned well on all sides. In a large casserole place the meat, 2 cups each cubed white potatoes and yams, 4 cups sliced onions, and 1 can mushrooms, drained (save the liquid). In the skillet blend ½ cup hot water, the reserved mushroom liquid, 1 can chicken soup, 1½ tablespoons brown sugar, 1 cup cold water, 2 teaspoons sea salt, and ½ teaspoon pepper. Heat until bubbly and pour over the contents of the casserole. Over the top place 1 can onion rings (or the equivalent in frozen fried onion rings). Bake in a 350°F. oven for 2½ to 3 hours, covered. Test the meat to see if it is tender after 2 hours and leave the cover off from then on.

GREEN PEPPER CARIBOU STEAK

This is a quick meal that improves in flavor and speed if you prepare the meat up through cooking ahead of time, then reheat just long enough to cook the vegetables at mealtime.

Cut 1 pound caribou round steak into ¼-inch-thick strips 2 inches long. In a bowl large enough to marinate the meat, combine ¼ cup soy sauce, 1 clove garlic, minced, 1½ teaspoons fresh ginger, minced (or ½ teaspoon ground ginger), and 1 tablespoon oil (a teaspoon of dark sesame oil adds a flavor we like, but it's optional). Add the meat, toss, and set aside.

Prepare 1 cup onion, cut into 1-inch wedges and then separated at the ring, 1 cup green pepper chunks, and 1 cup sliced or quartered mushrooms.

Heat 3 tablespoons oil in a large frying pan, add the drained meat (reserving the marinade), and stir-fry over high heat until tender, usually about 8 minutes. Add the vegetables and continue stir-frying until the onions and peppers are tender-crisp. Mix 1 tablespoon cornstarch in ¼ cup cold water and add to the marinade. Pour over the meat during the last 5 minutes of cooking. Accompany with steamed rice. This amount serves 4 and is easily doubled.

MOOSEBURGER WITH ONIONS

There are several methods for preparing super burger sandwiches from gameburger but this is just about our favorite. Use whole wheat bread or sourdough burger buns that you have baked.

If available, use sweet onions for this recipe. Remove outer skins and thinly slice one medium-size onion per sandwich. Have ready a heavy frying pan in which you have melted margarine or butter — 1 level tablespoon for each onion to be cooked. Over medium heat cook and stir the onions until they are golden brown. Push them to one side and put your burger in the space left.

The mooseburger should be extra lean and dusted with whole wheat flour. Season the burger with the usual salt and pepper, and also thyme, marjoram, and any other seasonings that you wish. (We usually add a small bit of beef soup base to the meat, too). Plop it into the pan and sauté it quickly, first on one side and then the other. You might put a little paprika on each side to help it brown. Cook it rare, medium, or well done as you like it.

Have your bread or bun ready. Place the burger on one piece and pile the onions on top. Close the sandwich and partially wrap it in a doubled-over paper towel. You should not need butter on this. We call this a "burger-in-a-blanket."

CHILIBURGERS DELUXE

Kids seem to love these burgers, so they must taste good. They are certainly easy to prepare, and leftovers can be reheated and used, too.

In a large, heavy skillet heat a little olive oil over medium heat. Put in about 1 pound of mooseburger or cariburger and crumble with a fork. Add 1 chopped onion and brown the mixture, stirring as it cooks. Stir in a can of chili beef soup and ½ cup water. Cook for 20 minutes, or until much of the liquid is absorbed. Serve on split burger buns and top with grated Cheddar cheese.

MOOSE OR CARIBOU CASSEROLE STEAK

Game round steak is the meat for this extra good casserole. Cut it in thick, serving-size pieces. You will probably need more pieces than you think because people will be coming back for more. Count on about 1½ hours cooking time.

Dredge the thick pieces of moose or caribou in the following mixture: whole wheat flour, beef soup base, pepper, thyme, paprika, chervil, and any other herbs or spices you fancy. The pieces of meat should be thoroughly coated, then put into a heavy frying pan (or 2 pans) coated with ⅛ inch of oil. The oil should be hot, but not smoking hot. Brown the pieces well on both sides. Sprinkle more of the dredging mixture on them and add a little warm water; cover tightly. Cook over low heat until most of the liquid is absorbed. Turn the pieces.

Again sprinkle some of the dredging material on the meat and add water. Repeat this turning and flouring process several times. After the first couple of times you can transfer the meat to a large, shallow casserole dish and cook it in the oven, meanwhile repeating the flouring and cooking down procedure at intervals. This should result in a thick brown gravy. We vary this occasionally by squirting

a little tomato paste into the casserole during the cooking (stir it up a bit then), or slicing an onion or two over the whole works. Garlic granules can also be added and sometimes even a bit of dry mustard, ginger, or curry powder. As usual, taste-test as you go along. If you used enough of the soup base you will not need any more salt.

SMOTHERED MOOSE FLANK STEAK

Some hunters just put the flank steak in with the burger meat and grind it up, but we like to prepare this smothered flank and wouldn't think of allowing it to be made into burger. Flank is tougher than some steaks, and will probably require at least 2 hours cooking time.

Be sure all natural fat is removed from the steak. Make shallow cuts about an inch apart diagonally on the steak and do likewise on the other side. Rub whole wheat flour into both sides of the meat and brown it in margarine in a heavy frying pan. After it is well browned, cut the flank into 2-inch strips while it is still in the frying pan. Sprinkle with a little flour, thyme, marjoram, chervil, pepper, and vegetable seasoning, if you have it. Pour on a small amount of warm water. Add a tablespoon of beef soup base and a couple of squirts from the tomato paste tube. You probably won't need any more salt, but taste the gravy after it has cooked awhile and correct the seasoning if it needs it. You should sprinkle on more flour and turn the meat several times until a thick brown gravy forms. The steak can finish cooking in the oven, if you like. Be sure the meat is fork tender before you remove it from the heat source.

For a good variation, we sometimes add a small handful of dried bell pepper pieces or new baby carrots fresh from the garden.

CHILI

No two cooks make chili in the same way. It can be simple with only meat, beans, tomatoes, and chili powder in it besides the liquid or it can contain up to 30 or even more ingredients. So let your imagination loose on this one. Incidentally, chili is even better when it's reheated or when it is frozen and then heated another day.

We like to dice a thin slice of salt pork, fry it to a crisp, and then crumble mooseburger into the fat in the pan. Brown the burger by stirring it and turning it frequently as it cooks. Have ready as many cooked red beans (by bulk) as you have burger and stir them into the meat. You may need to transfer the material to a larger kettle at this point. Add the water the beans were cooked in, as well as a can of tomato purée or canned tomatoes cut in pieces, tomato paste, and tomato sauce. Use at least two forms of tomato in this dish.

Add a generous dollop of beef soup base, 1 or 2 tablespoons brown sugar, pepper, bell pepper dices, jalapeño peppers (dried, canned, or fresh), cayenne pepper (go easy on this), plenty of chili powder, cumin, thyme, and marjoram. We usually add a little diced crystallized ginger, dried celery flakes, dry mustard, and lots of chopped onion. A little garlic, either fresh or dried, would not be amiss either.

Let all this bubble and simmer along for a couple of hours or more, stirring from time to time and like-

wise testing occasionally to see how it tastes. You may need to correct the seasoning or add more water.

CHICKEN-FRIED MOOSE STEAK

A good way to cook steaks that are not quite as tender as you would like. Really tough ones should not be treated in this fashion, though. Sometimes we even use sirloin tips or T-bones in this manner. Caribou, sheep, and goat steaks can be prepared this way, too.

Trim all the natural fat off of a round or shoulder moose steak. Pound whole wheat flour into the steak with the edge of a heavy plate. Fry in a heavy skillet in margarine over medium heat. Sprinkle a little thyme, minced garlic, salt, pepper, and paprika on each side of the steak as you turn it. (The paprika will aid in browning the steaks.) Fry until the steak is as done as you like it.

The drippings in the pan can be the base for an excellent gravy. Just add a little beef soup base, pepper, and a tablespoon or two of flour, depending on how much fat is still left in the pan. Scrape and stir until well mixed. Pour in a cup or so of milk and cook, stirring, until thickened. If the gravy is too thick for your taste just add more milk, a few spoonfuls at a time.

BLIND PIGEONS

Blind Pigeons is just another name for cabbage rolls, and these are really good ones. The proportions here can be varied to suit; some prefer more rice and some like more meat in their rolls. All seasonings should be adjusted to taste.

Steam a large head of loose-leaf cabbage until the 6 or 8 outside leaves can be easily removed. (It helps to core the cabbage part way before steaming.) Drain the removed outer leaves on paper towels and cool. Mix together 1½ pounds mooseburger or cariburger, ⅔ cup white rice, cooked and drained, 1 small onion, chopped, and any seasonings you wish. Put about 6 tablespoons of the mixture on each cabbage leaf. Roll the leaves up tightly. Place the rolls in a 6-quart pot and cover with canned tomatoes, plus 1 can water. Cook over medium heat for about 2 hours.   *– Nancy Sadusky*

CHEESY MOOSE-TOMATO PIE

Many times we have stolen excellent recipes from food packages, and this is one example. The original recipe called for beef, but we like moose just as well and maybe better in the pie.

From a 6-ounce package of Brownberry Onion & Garlic Croutons set aside 1 cup of croutons. In a small bowl mix ½ cup hot water and 1 egg with the remaining croutons; stir to combine. Press the crouton mixture into a greased 9-inch pie pan. Combine 1 pound extra lean mooseburger or any other ground game, 1 cup shredded Cheddar cheese, ¼ cup barbecue sauce, 1 egg, 2 teaspoons instant minced onion, and the reserved cup of croutons. Press into the crust. Place 6 or 7 thick tomato slices on top.

Bake at 400°F. for 20 to 30 minutes. Top with ½ cup shredded Cheddar cheese; bake for 2 minutes longer.

STUFFED HEART

Stuffed moose or caribou heart makes an acceptable holiday dinner entrée and is usually more easily obtained on the homestead than turkey. It is not as large as a turkey, though, and you may need something else to fill in, but that should be easy with a well-stocked freezer.

Trim all of the fat from the heart. Remove the blood vessels and membranes from it and wash thoroughly with cold water. Wipe dry with paper towels. Rub inside and out with salt, pepper, and garlic powder. Stuff tightly and pack extra stuffing around the heart in a shallow roasting pan. Follow the Corn Bread Stuffing recipe as described in the Tail Ends chapter (p. 91).

Preheat the oven to 350°F. Lay 2 or 3 strips of bacon over the heart and cover loosely with foil. Bake for 1½ hours, then remove the foil so that the meat may brown a bit. Bake for another half hour. When ready to serve, slice the meat on the diagonal. Serve with Currant Jelly (p. 69).

KIDNEYS IN TOMATO SAUCE

Many people discard the kidneys of big game, but by so doing they miss a nourishing treat. Remember, though, that kidneys toughen if cooked too long.

Heat 3 tablespoons olive oil or other cooking oil in a frying pan. Sauté 1 cup minced wild chives (or onions) for about 10 minutes. Add 1 teaspoon sea salt, ¾ cup tomato sauce (or the equivalent in tomato paste), and 1 cup sliced puffball mushrooms. (You may use mushrooms purchased from the market if puffballs are not in season.) Cook over low heat for 10 minutes.

Meanwhile remove the skin and fat from the kidneys of moose or caribou (or other game); discard the core and slice the kidneys thinly.

Melt 3 tablespoons butter or margarine in the same skillet with the above ingredients and cook the sliced kidneys in it for about 2 minutes over medium heat. Add 2 cups green peas, ½ teaspoon pepper, 1 tablespoon minced parsley, ¼ cup dry white wine, and 1½ teaspoons salt. Continue cooking for 2 minutes longer, or until kidneys are tender. Serve with rice.

MEATBALLS

These meatballs can be made from any big game burger. We usually have either moose or cariburger on hand, so that is what we use most. You can vary the seasoning to suit your taste. You can also use a little tomato juice in place of some of the water, if you like, or a few squirts from the tomato paste tube. This is another recipe that invites experimentation. It makes a dozen or more meatballs.

Follow the cooking instructions on a 5-ounce package of Uncle Ben's rice, but use only about one-third of the package. Cook the rice until tender and fluffy. In the meantime, crumble 1½ pounds of burger into a bowl, add seasonings of your choice, then stir in the cooked rice. Break an egg into the bowl and stir gently to mix all the ingredients well. Pour about ¼ cup olive oil into a large, heavy frying pan and place over medium heat. With floured hands, form balls about 2 inches in diameter and place them in the hot frying pan. Do not put the meatballs too close together; you may have to cook them in 2 batches. Cook until browned on all sides. Sprinkle

with a very little flour (preferably whole wheat) and pour on a little water. Cover the pan tightly. Cook again until the moisture is gone. Sprinkle with flour again and again add a little water and cover. Repeat this process several times.

The meatballs seem to taste even better if cooked for the last few turnings in the oven. Long, slow cooking is the secret to this recipe. A good variation calls for sliced onions to be added to the pan after the first browning. After the cooked meatballs have been removed to a heated serving dish, scrape the "goodie" loose from the bottom of the pan and add some hot water. While the water comes to a boil, add a tablespoon of beef soup base. Make a paste of flour and cold water and stir it in to thicken the gravy. Mashed potatoes are a natural complement to this dish.

BURGER-STUFFED PEPPERS

My mother used to grind up leftover beef roast to use for stuffing peppers. She would sometimes stuff onions, too, and both recipes were excellent. We seldom eat beef and rarely have leftover game roast, so for stuffed peppers we generally use gameburger.

Remove the stem ends of green bell peppers. Take out the seeds and remove the white membrane from the inside. Cook in boiling water for 5 or 6 minutes, drain thoroughly, and allow to cool. Meanwhile mix the stuffing.

Cook 1 cup of Uncle Ben's rice according to package directions and allow to cool a bit. Chop 1 small onion rather fine and fry it with ½ to ¾ pound gameburger in 2 tablespoons margarine or butter. Stir with the back of a pancake turner to keep every-

thing moving in the pan. Cook just until the onion begins to brown. Stir into the meat mixture any seasonings you like. Add the cooked rice, a couple of squirts from the tomato paste tube, and a little beef soup base. Stuff the peppers and set them in a shallow pan. Melt 1 tablespoon margarine and stir into it a few fine dry bread crumbs. Sprinkle the crumbs on top of the stuffed peppers. Place the pan in a preheated 350°F. oven and bake for 15 to 20 minutes. Turn the oven heat up to 400°F. and bake until the crumbs are browned.

CRUNCHY MEATBALLS

These crunchy meatballs can be used as hors d'oeuvres or as a dinner entrée.

Place 1 large egg, ¼ cup milk, 1 medium-size sweet onion, 2 tablespoons catsup, 1 large garlic clove, 1 teaspoon sea salt, ¼ teaspoon chili powder, 1 teaspoon chervil, and 1 tablespoon Worcestershire sauce in the blender. Blend until thoroughly mixed. Then mix in 1 to 1¼ pounds gameburger (beef can be substituted if you must), and 1 cup fine dry bread crumbs. Mold into small balls about the size of cherries. Fry in deep fat heated to 375°F.; they cook quickly. Fry only a few meatballs at a time so that the fat bubbles freely around the tiny balls. Drain on several thicknesses of paper towels.

SAUCE FOR MEATBALLS
Blend ½ cup catsup, 1 small clove

garlic, minced, and ¼ cup water. Put 2 tablespoons margarine in a saucepan; add the blended ingredients and ½ cup white wine. Simmer about 5 minutes. Serve as a hot dip for the little meatballs.

STUFFED FLANK STEAK

For this recipe you can use flank steak from any big game — moose, elk, or caribou would be our choice. Other game flanks are usually too small for stuffing.

Pound the steak thin with the edge of a heavy plate; rub with sea salt, pepper, and thyme. Place in a flat dish and add ½ cup snipped wild chives (onions may be substituted), 2 tablespoons minced parsley, and ¼ to ½ cup wine vinegar. Marinate in the refrigerator overnight, basting and turning the steak occasionally.

Soak 4 slices of bread in ½ cup milk; drain and mash until smooth. Mix the bread with 2 cups finely chopped wild greens (dandelions, nettles, fireweed, goosefoot or goosetongue, etc.); be sure the greens are young so they won't be bitter. Add 4 tablespoons grated Cheddar cheese and 6 slices of bacon that have been fried, drained, and crumbled. Taste-test for seasoning and make any necessary adjustments.

Spread the mixture on the drained marinated steak and roll it up like a jelly roll. Tie the roll with heavy cord to help it keep its shape. Heat 3 tablespoons olive or other cooking oil in a casserole or Dutch oven and lightly brown the meat in it, turning the roll frequently so that all sides are browned evenly. Barely cover the meat with boiling water and add a bay leaf. Cover and simmer gently for 3 hours, or until the meat is tender.

Drain and place a weight on the roll. Chill; slice thinly for serving. The liquid drained off may be saved for soup or gravy.

ALASKA SCRAPPLE

Here is an excellent breakfast dish. Serve it with blueberry syrup, a couple of slices of crisp bacon, and a good cup of coffee and you will have a world-beater.

Use scrap or shoulder meat of any big game. Cover meat with water and cook until tender, adding an onion for extra flavor. Drain off the liquid and measure. Grind the meat. Use 1½ quarts broth for each quart of meat. Add water to the broth if necessary to make the required amount. Put the broth in a large saucepan over high heat. Stir in 1 cup of cornmeal for each quart of liquid. Sprinkle it on the boiling liquid by hand to avoid lumping. Reduce the heat to low and simmer for half an hour. Add the ground meat and season with salt and pepper. A wooden spoon should be used for stirring this concoction. Simmer the mixture until it is quite thick.

Pour into loaf pans to cool and harden. To serve, slice thinly, roll in flour, and fry until lightly browned on both sides. Serve hot with syrup and butter, too, if desired.

ONION SOUP

Onion soup is always good, but it is much better when made with moose stock for the liquid. If sweet onions are available the sugar called for in the recipe below will not be needed.

Melt 3 or 4 tablespoons butter or margarine in a large, heavy saucepan. Add 1 tablespoon olive oil and slowly cook about 5 cups chopped onion and 1 teaspoon finely slivered crystallized

ginger, together with 1 to 2 teaspoons salt and ½ teaspoon sugar. Continue cooking slowly for 25 to 35 minutes, stirring often, until the onions have turned light brown. Add 3 tablespoons flour, 1 tablespoon at a time, stirring after each addition. Cook for 4 or 5 minutes more. Add 8 cups strong moose stock, about 2 cups at a time, stirring after each addition. Add ½ cup dry white vermouth and simmer slowly, partially covered, for about 45 minutes. Stir occasionally and skim as needed. Taste and correct seasoning; serve very hot.

GINGERED GAME STRIPS

Sheep, goat, caribou, or moose — any of these will be fine for gingered strips. In fact you could use a combination if you cared to.

Using a rolling pin, crush finely about 18 gingersnaps that have been placed in a large plastic bag. Add 2 pounds of game shoulder strips, cut about ½ inch wide and 3 inches long. Shake the bag until the strips are evenly coated with crumbs. In a large, heavy skillet cook the game strips in hot oil until lightly browned on both sides. Add 1 can (10½ ounces) condensed onion soup, undiluted, ⅔ cup water, and ½ cup cider vinegar. Bring to a boil, then reduce the heat, cover, and simmer until the meat is tender, about 30 minutes. Add any remaining crumbs from the bag and simmer another minute or two. Serve with mashed potatoes or whole wheat noodles.

ALASKAN BROILED STEAK

Steak broiled to perfection seems to be the favored method of preparation for many people. A good cut of almost any game will broil well, although we prefer moose or caribou.

Select a good steak — 1 to 1½ inches thick. Rub with salt and pepper and any other seasonings your fancy dictates, but keep it simple. Rub the grid of a broiling rack with suet to prevent sticking. Preheat the broiler for 15 minutes. Place the steak 5 inches below the heat source and sear quickly to prevent loss of juices. Turn several times. A medium-rare steak requires approximately 15 minutes broiling. Serve on hot plates with a dab of butter or margarine on top of each steak. Try these with garlic bread and a tossed green salad — nothing more is needed.

PAN-FRIED MOOSE STEAK

This is a winner among steaks! Other big game steaks besides those carved from a moose can be substituted, but we like moose best.

Moose steak about 1 inch thick or a bit less is just fine for this. Pour just barely enough vegetable oil into a hot cast-iron frying pan to coat the bottom, adding more later if necessary. Heat until the fat begins to smoke. Have the steak already dredged in flour and shake off any surplus. (If there is reason to think the steak may not be tender enough, it may be scored lightly or pounded with the flat of a cleaver before dredging.)

Place the steak in the pan and reduce the heat to medium at once. Cook until brown, turn quickly, and brown the other side, too. Continue turning about every 45 seconds until the steak reaches the degree of doneness you prefer. Season to taste after the third or fourth turning. Remove

42

the steak to a hot plate and keep it hot until the gravy is ready. Be sure to scrape up the residue in the bottom of the pan and use it as the gravy base. Just add a tablespoon or two of margarine and a tablespoon of flour; then pour in 1 cup milk. Cook, stirring, until the gravy thickens and serve with potatoes and the steak.

SHEEP MOUNTAINS

Sheep Mountains are simply mountain sheep croquettes formed into triangular "mountain" shapes before frying in deep fat. Any big game, game bird, fish, or even shellfish can be prepared in this way. It is a fine way to dispose of leftovers, and the variations are unlimited. For a binder try canned soup, White Sauce (p. 91), gravy, cream, or what have you. Vary the seasonings, too. This is a basic recipe for your guidance, so don't be afraid to make changes in it.

Mix together 2 cups of flaked or finely chopped cooked meat and a few drops of onion juice (or lemon juice if you are using seafood). Add salt, pepper, and any other seasonings you wish. Mix well, then add just enough thick White Sauce (p. 91) to moisten the mixture, but not so much that it will lose its shape when molded with your hands. Form into mountain shapes about 1 inch thick and 3 inches to a side. Of course, the meat may be shaped into more conventional shapes like balls, sticks, or rolls. Dip the mountains in beaten egg and then coat them carefully in fine dry bread crumbs. Fry in deep fat heated to 375°F. and drain well on paper towels.

If you have plenty of meat, make up a lot of these; after they have been well drained and completely cooled, wrap them in meal-size bundles of foil and freeze. About 45 minutes before you want to serve them, remove the bundle from the freezer and heat in a 350°F. oven without removing the foil.

Sheep Mountains are best served with a thick White Sauce, enriched with various herbs, dribbled over their tops.

CURRIED MOUNTAIN SHEEP

The amount of curry you use in this dish depends upon your fondness for curry as a flavoring. Serve with white rice as it is done in the Orient.

Cut the meat of mountain sheep into 1-inch cubes and brown in a little oil in a hot cast-iron skillet. When well browned, remove the meat from the pan. Add 2 or 3 tablespoons of flour to the drippings in the pan and stir until the flour is browned. Add half of a medium-size onion, finely chopped, ½ to 1 teaspoon curry powder, ½ teaspoon salt, a dash of pepper, and a little beef soup base. Mix well and bring slowly to a boil. Return the meat to the pan and reduce the heat to simmer. Add a dash of lemon juice. Cook until the meat is tender.

WILD GAME CHINO

Stir-fried game with a slightly Oriental flavor, this recipe can be varied in many ways. Instead of meat try shrimp sometime and use snow peas in place of the green beans — but try the recipe below first.

Cut moose meat in strips ½ inch wide by 2 inches long. Brown the strips, using the usual hot skillet with its bottom just barely coated with oil. Use approximately 1½ to 2 cups of

meat, according to the number of persons to be served. When the meat is slightly browned, add 1 large onion chopped fine, 1 to 1½ cups green beans, canned or frozen, 1 green pepper, cut in narrow strips (or its equivalent in dehydrated peppers), and 1 cup diced celery.

Cook about 5 minutes, meanwhile combining 2 tablespoons cornstarch, 1½ tablespoons soy sauce, 1 cup liquid (juice from the mushrooms plus water), and salt and pepper to taste. Now add 1 cup mushrooms, frozen or canned. Add all this to the meat mixture. Cook until the liquid is clear, stirring slowly as it cooks. It should appear shiny when cooked enough. Serve with fluffy white rice and garnish with strips of pimiento and a few sprigs of parsley.

BRAISED VENISON

Sometimes a deer has lived too long to yield tender steaks and roasts, and that is when we must resort to braising.

Cut the venison into serving-size pieces and dredge with whole wheat flour. Season with salt, pepper, and any other seasonings you wish. Thyme and marjoram are both good here, as well as dried bell pepper pieces and minced onions. Sometimes we use a squirt or two from the tomato paste tube, too. All of these seasonings can be added as the meat cooks.

Heat about ¼ inch of fat in a Dutch oven and brown the meat slowly in the fat, turning the pieces to ensure even browning. Then put a rack under the meat, add about ¼ cup water, and cover the pan tightly. Continue cooking over low heat or in a slow oven (300°F.) until tender (about 1½ to 2

hours). Add a little more water from time to time if necessary to keep the venison from scorching.

GERMAN-ALASKAN POTATO SOUP WITH DUMPLINGS

This recipe was given to me a long time ago by a German friend; I gave it an Alaskan twist by substituting moose for beef in the soup. The dumplings I have never modified; they are quite wonderful as they are.

Take a couple of pounds of one of the tougher cuts of moose and cut it into bite-size pieces. Brown the chunks quickly in a hot skillet, then put them in a large pan, cover with water, season to taste, add some diced onion, and simmer until tender. When the meat is nearly done, add 6 peeled and diced potatoes and several peeled and sliced carrots. Continue cooking until the vegetables are soft. In another pan melt 2 tablespoons butter and blend in 3 tablespoons flour; combine with 1 cup water, stirring constantly. Pour that mixture into the soup and blend well. Bring the soup to a boil and then reduce the heat and taste to see if any more seasonings are called for.

DUMPLINGS

Scald ½ cup milk. Dissolve 1 package yeast in 2 tablespoons warm water; let stand for 5 minutes. Combine in a large bowl ¼ cup butter or margarine, 2 tablespoons sugar, and ¼ teaspoon salt. Immediately pour the warm milk over this mixture; when the mixture is lukewarm, blend in 1 cup flour and beat until smooth. Stir in the dissolved yeast and mix well.

Measure 2 to 2½ cups of flour. Add

half the flour to the yeast mixture and beat until smooth. Blend in 2 well-beaten eggs. Add enough of the remaining flour to make a soft dough. Turn the dough out onto a lightly floured surface and let stand for 5 to 10 minutes. Then knead the dough, form it into a ball, put it in a greased bowl, cover, and let rise until double in bulk. Turn the dough out onto a floured surface and divide it into 8 balls. Cover the balls loosely with a clean kitchen towel and let them rise until double in bulk again.

To cook the dumplings you will need a heavy skillet that has a tight-fitting lid. Put 1½ cups water and 1 tablespoon butter or margarine in the skillet. Arrange the 8 dumplings in the skillet, not too close together. Put the cover on and cook over high heat for just a few minutes, until you see steam rising from under the lid. Be careful not to burn the bottoms of the dumplings. Reduce the heat and cook 30 minutes, or until the steaming stops. Do not remove the skillet lid while the dumplings are steaming. Carefully remove the dumplings from the skillet and serve with the hot potato soup.   – Twila Leask

SPLENDID SPAGHETTI

Spaghetti and macaroni both work well in this recipe; whichever you have on hand is the one to use.

Cook about a pound of spaghetti according to the directions on the box. Meanwhile pan-fry a pound of any kind of gameburger and season it with salt, pepper, chopped onion or snipped wild chives, and other seasonings to taste. When the meat is cooked and well browned, combine it with the cooked and drained spaghetti. Stir in a can of chopped pimientos and a good handful of broiled or pan-fried wild mushrooms (you can also use a can of mushroom stems and pieces, drained). Pour in 1 can (10½ ounces) cream of mushroom soup and 1 can of water. Mix well but gently. Place in a baking dish and bake in a 325°F. oven for 30 minutes or a bit longer. To vary, add 1 small can of chopped ripe olives with the mushrooms.

MOOSEBURGER PIZZA

Preparing this homemade pizza takes more time than dropping in at your local pizza parlor, but it is different from any you can buy and it makes a welcome change. This recipe will make 2 good-sized pizzas.

First get the dough going. Measure 6 cups of flour (either all unbleached white flour or 4 cups white and 2 cups whole wheat flour) into a large bowl. In a separate container combine 1½ cups buttermilk, 4 tablespoons butter or margarine, 4 tablespoons honey, and ½ teaspoon salt. Heat the buttermilk mixture to lukewarm. Dissolve 1 package yeast in ¼ cup warm water. Add the yeast and milk mixture to the flour and combine to make a firm dough. Turn out the dough and knead for about 5 minutes, or until it is smooth and elastic. Put the dough in a greased bowl, cover, and let rise until double in bulk (about 1 hour).

While the dough is rising, prepare the toppings. Grate plenty of cheese — mostly mozzarella, but also Cheddar, jack, or others if you like. Chop some onions and some wild chives if you have some handy. Fry about a

pound of mooseburger, crumbling it as you fry.

When the dough has risen, punch it down, divide it in half, and roll out the two parts to fit your baking sheets; the dough should be about ¼ inch thick — how thick depends on how thick you like pizza crust. Let the rolled-out dough rise for about 15 minutes. Then spread a generous amount of pizza sauce on the dough. I buy prepared sauce, but you can make it yourself. Sprinkle on plenty of oregano, garlic powder, pepper, a little thyme, and any other spices that sound good to you. Put on a goodly amount of grated cheese and top with the crumbled mooseburger.

Bake in a 350°F. oven for 20 to 30 minutes, depending on how thick the crust is and how crispy you like it.

– A. Friend

CAMPFIRE BARBECUED RIBS

The rib section is one part of big game that cools off quickly enough to be used in camp before the hunters head for home. Here is one way it is done.

Leave the rack of ribs intact. Rub with oil or bacon fat and roast both sides near a hot bed of coals. The rack should be propped vertically with the meaty side to the top and should have a backing of heavy-duty aluminum foil. Cooking time will depend on the thickness of the meat. When nearly done, cover the rack with the following barbecue sauce and continue cooking until done.

BARBECUE SAUCE

Combine 1 cup tomato catsup, ½ to 1 cup Highbush Cranberry Catsup, (p. 74), 1 large onion, chopped fine, chopped garlic or garlic powder, 1 tablespoon Worcestershire sauce, 2 tablespoons chili powder, celery salt, ¼ cup oil, and ¼ cup vinegar.

MOOSEBURGER LASAGNA

This one requires a couple of 3-quart baking dishes. The extra dish freezes well and is nice to have on hand.

Brown 2½ pounds mooseburger in ¾ cup olive oil in a skillet. Drain, leaving a little fat in the skillet. Add 2 medium (or 1 large) onions, chopped, 3 or 4 cloves of garlic, chopped, two 12-ounce cans tomato paste, three 8-ounce cans tomato sauce, 2 cups water (to dilute the tomato paste), 3 teaspoons salt, 1½ teaspoons pepper, 6 bay leaves, and a little chopped parsley. Simmer over low heat for ½ hour. You will also need 2¼ pounds mozzarella or Monterey jack cheese and 2 pounds ricotta or small-curd cottage cheese. Meanwhile cook 1½ boxes (24-ounce size) lasagna noodles, following cooking directions on the box. In the baking dishes layer the sauce, lasagna noodles, mozzarella or Monterey jack cheese, and ricotta or cottage cheese. Repeat the layers, estimating amounts so that the layers come out even. Garnish with some mozzarella and ¾ cup grated Parmesan cheese. Bake in a 375°F. oven with a foil cover for about 30 minutes. Let the lasagna sit for a few minutes after removing it from the oven to facilitate serving.

– Richard Hull

MOUNTAIN MAN'S SHISH KEBABS

Sheep meat is called for here, but any big game meat that is tender and good can be used.

Marinate 1-inch cubes of mountain sheep meat overnight in the following: ¼ cup wine vinegar (or lowbush cranberry juice), ½ cup salad oil, and ¼ teaspoon each garlic salt, onion salt, celery salt, and cracked pepper. Be sure there is enough of the liquid to cover the meat cubes completely. Stir occasionally. When ready to barbecue the kebabs, thread them on long skewers or "weenie" sticks, alternating the meat with tiny raw onions, green pepper squares, mushrooms, etc. Cook over your campfire or charcoal grill until done enough to suit you. People will be asking for seconds on these, so have them ready.

CARIBOU RUMP ROAST

Any of the big game animals should provide you with a good rump roast, but we usually try to make this recipe with caribou meat.

Select a good cut — about 4 to 5 pounds — from the rump of the caribou. Preheat the oven to 350°F. Rub the meat with a bit of seasoned flour, being sure to cover all portions with the flour. Shake off any excess and place the roast on a rack in a roasting pan. Cover tightly and roast for about 45 minutes. While it is roasting, prepare a basting sauce of bacon drippings, finely chopped onions or chives, and a little of your best meat sauce. Simmer this mixture for a few minutes and add to it a little beef soup base. After the first 45 minutes of cooking, baste the roast with the

sauce at 15-minute intervals and continue roasting until it tests tender when pierced with a fork. Bake for an additional 15 or 20 minutes with the cover removed. Serve the pan drippings as a sauce.

ROAST MOUNTAIN GOAT

We don't get mountain goat often — only if someone brings it to us. The hunter gets more meat for the time spent when he goes after moose or caribou, although there is nothing the matter with the meat of mountain goat. You can prepare mountain sheep this way, too.

Choose about a 5-pound roast from the round. Rub it well with salt and pepper. (Onion salt is good instead of the standard salt if you wish to try it.) Place the meat on a rack in a shallow roasting pan. Cover the roast with a thin coating of prepared Dijon-style mustard. Bake in a 350°F. oven for about 3 hours, or until the roast is done enough for you.

For a different taste, try coating the meat liberally with applesauce or with unpeeled tart apple slices. Mountain sheep will probably take about half an hour less baking time than mountain goat.

MEDIUM-FAMOUS ORCA JONES VEGETABLE MESS

Tim Jones, who is a charter boat skipper, says this is a good one-dish meal for a small stove. It is also great warmed up and added to. If some is left over, it's fine for breakfast.

Take one potato for each person you expect to feed, slice for frying, and put in a big frying pan with butter. Add a sliced onion, chives, and pepper. Cook until the potatoes are soft, but

not hard-fried. Any number of seasonings can now be added. When the potatoes are ready throw in a vegetable. I like fresh broccoli for this, with cauliflower as second choice, but just about any vegetable will do. The broccoli, though, adds a nice green touch. Cover and cook until the vegetable is warmed through, stirring once in a while. Keep the vegetable crisp. Once cooked, put slices of cheese on top. I like to use Tillamook medium Cheddar. Cover the pan again. Let the cheese melt down through the whole mess and serve. It's a good rib-sticking complement to any meat and leaves a lot of room to put in whatever you might have lying around as leftovers. Leftover game or fish can be cut into bite-size pieces and added, too.

– Tim "Orca" Jones

VENISON GOULASH

Goulash is an Old World dish that has found favor with a lot of us. In Europe it is most often made with lamb, but venison substitutes nicely.

Cut about 3 pounds venison stew meat into 1-inch chunks and dredge with flour, salt, and pepper. Melt ½ cup butter or margarine in a large casserole and brown the meat, a few pieces at a time. Be careful not to allow the fat to burn. Sprinkle paprika generously over the meat as it cooks. Add 4 cups sliced onions. Seed and slice 1 green pepper and add it along with 1 bay leaf and 1½ to 2 cups strong game stock. Cover the casserole and simmer until the meat is tender (about an hour). This last part may be done in the oven if you prefer. About 5 minutes before you take the goulash off the heat (or out of the

oven) skim off all the fat. Stir in a little vodka if you like. Serve over rice or whole wheat noodles.

MOOSE JAMBALAYA

Coriss Dossman has transformed Louisiana dishes into Alaskan ones. He just substitutes our game for the protein called for originally. He makes use of seasonings from his Creole and Cajun seasoning shop.

Brown ½ pound bacon until crisp in a heavy 6-quart pot. Remove the bacon, crumble, and set aside. Leave the drippings in the pot. Chop 2 medium-size onions and sauté them until dark golden brown. Add 2 ribs of celery, chopped, 1 cup chopped parsley, 1 medium bell pepper, chopped, 1 teaspoon garlic powder, and ½ cup chopped green onion tops. Cook for about 10 minutes.

Sprinkle in salt and Chinese red pepper to taste. Add 8 cups water, 2 teaspoons Kitchen Bouquet, and the reserved bacon bits. Toss in 2 pounds of diced moose meat as soon as the mixture begins to boil. Cook over medium heat for 10 minutes, then add 4 cups of uncooked long-grain rice.

Cook for another 10 minutes, then cover and cook until the rice is tender. Stir once to allow the juices to spread evenly throughout.

– Coriss Dossman

MEATBALL SOUP

Breadsticks (p. 83) are just the thing to serve with this soup. Those sourdough breadsticks are extra special with most any soup.

Put 3 quarts of soup stock in a large kettle and simmer slowly. Combine ½

pound cariburger with 1 beaten egg, ¼ cup fine dry bread crumbs, ¼ cup finely chopped onion, and any other seasonings you wish. Blend well and, if the mixture is too moist to form compact balls, add a few more crumbs. Shape into tiny (½- to ¾-inch diameter) meatballs and drop into the gently bubbling stock in the kettle. Continue to simmer for 30 to 45 minutes. If you like, add any leftover vegetables, or canned ones, a few minutes before removing the soup from the heat.

MESQUITE MOOSE STEAKS

You'll want at least two moose steaks — cut about ¾ inch thick — for each person. We've never seen anyone eat fewer than two at a sitting.

Dip the steaks in cooking oil and season with plenty of pepper, garlic powder, and a little salt. If the steaks are tough, use some meat tenderizer and no salt.

To grill these steaks you'll need a covered charcoal grill; the cover is important because the mesquite smoke penetrates the meat better if the smoke is trapped by a cover. Light the grill and wait until the coals are hot. Then toss on a few mesquite chips. Put the steaks on the grill, sear them quickly, and then put the cover on the grill. The steaks cook quickly (roughly 4 or 5 minutes). Make sure they don't overcook — it's best to leave them a bit rare.   *– John Sadusky*

BURGER SHORTCAKE

You don't have to have fruit to make shortcake! Just try some good game-burger in place of the ~~fruit if you~~ *want to serve it for dess* ~~ert. Who~~ *cares?*

Sauté 2 slices of bacon, diced; cho~~p a~~ small onion and cook just until the onion is golden. Next add about a pound of any gameburger and a nice variety of seasonings. We use, besides the usual salt and pepper, thyme, marjoram, vegetable seasoning, and often a *few* pieces of minced dried jalapeño pepper. Minced dried garlic is good here, too. Continue cooking until the meat is nicely browned, stirring and crumbling the burger as it cooks.

Blend in 2 tablespoons flour and then add a cup of water, ½ teaspoon prepared mustard, and ½ cup catsup. Bring to a boil, stirring. Remove from the heat, but keep warm.

Prepare your favorite baking-powder biscuit recipe and roll the dough to a ¼-inch thickness. Cut with a large cutter — about 3 inches in diameter. Place half of the biscuits on ungreased baking sheets and brush with melted butter or margarine. Now place the remaining biscuits on top. Bake in a preheated 425°F. oven for 12 to 15 minutes, or until well done and browned. To serve, lift off the top biscuits and pour meat filling over the bottoms. Replace the tops and pour a little of the filling over each top.

MOOSEBURGER PUDDING

In spite of its name this is not a dessert. You will need second helpings and there will be no room for dessert anyhow.

Crumble a pound, or a little more, of mooseburger into a saucepan and add ½ cup water. Cook over medium heat

medium-
onion to-
...ed moose-
...blespoons
...ne and ½ cup
...ixture. Beat 2
along with salt,
...ed bay leaf. Pour
into a ... baking dish and
bake uncovere... a 350°F. oven for
1½ hours.

MIXED BROIL

Use the bottom of the broiler pan for this one. The important thing is not to mash or bang on the meat the way you do when making ordinary hamburger patties; that will cause these little steaks to be dry and tough.

Lightly grease the pan. Divide 1½ pounds gameburger into 4 servings. Handling it as little as possible, gently push each piece into a more-or-less rounded shape. Sprinkle the tops with finely minced garlic. Use a fork to poke holes in the meat. Spoon on a little soy sauce and allow it to trickle down into the holes. Turn the steaks over, place in the broiler pan, and spoon on more soy sauce.

Broil about 5 inches under the heat source until the tops are brown (about 3 or 4 minutes). Turn the meat and push it toward the back of the pan. Add 1 sliced onion, 1 sliced medium zucchini, and 8 to 10 sliced mushrooms (wild or cultivated). Stir as you add them to coat them with the pan juices. You may need to add a little oil to the pan if the burger had little fat of its own. When the vegetables are coated well, spread them out in the pan. Broil an additional 3 or 4 minutes, until the vegetables and meat are done to taste. – *Jan Griffeth*

BURGER LOAF

For those people who love tomatoes in their cookery, this dish should provide just what they want.

Mix about 1½ pounds cariburger with 2 cups fine dry bread crumbs, ⅔ cup diced processed American cheese, 1 medium onion, minced, and half a green pepper, chopped fine. You can work in 2 teaspoons salt and other seasonings to taste. Combine a small can of tomato sauce with 2 beaten eggs and mix with the meat. Shape the mixture into 2 rounded loaves and place in a greased shallow baking pan. Bake at 350°F. for about an hour or until done clear through. Serve hot with tomato sauce or other meat sauce of your choice.

BURGER BALLS

Don't throw out that leftover mushroom soup or gravy. In fact, you might do well to make some extra of either of them purposely, just to use in Burger Balls.

Combine ¼ cup leftover mushroom gravy or mushroom soup with about a pound of gameburger of any kind. Add to the combination ¼ cup quick-cooking rice, 1 egg, ¼ cup bread crumbs and a handful of minced dried wild chives. Mix together well and shape into small balls — about an inch or so in diameter. Brown in a small amount of bacon drippings or other fat, then add another cup of the gravy or soup. Cover the skillet and simmer slowly for 45 minutes. This part of the cooking can be done in a slow oven if you so desire. Also, you can vary it with the addition of one or more vegetables such as sliced carrots, chopped peppers, coarsely diced potatoes, or green peas.

MOOSIBOU CAKES

As the name implies, these are made from either moose or caribou, but we prefer moose. Both make excellent eating and are easy to prepare.

With well-floured hands form seasoned ground moose or caribou into plump cakes about 1 inch thick and 2½ inches in diameter. They should be a cross between a burger and a meatball in size and shape. A tremendous improvement in the flavor can be made by adding chopped onions as you form the cakes. Sauté or fry in a hot, heavy skillet with a minimum of fat, margarine, oil, or drippings. Brown well on each side. Fry until medium-well done or more, turning several times as the cakes cook. Remove the cakes to a hot platter while you make the gravy. Stir enough cornstarch into the fat remaining in the pan to make a thin paste. Also add a little beef soup base. Stir and cook over medium-low heat, allowing the paste to brown a bit and scraping up any residue clinging to the bottom of the pan. Add 1 cup milk all at once and stir constantly until the gravy thickens. You will probably need to add more milk and continue stirring until the gravy reaches the consistency you like. This requires gentle simmering for several minutes. Season to taste. This is our favorite recipe for moose or caribou.

BROILED GAMEBURGER ROLLS

These are best if freshly baked sourdough French rolls (p. 84) are used, but other kinds will suffice. Also, a whole loaf of French bread can be used and the portions taken off in chunks when done.

You will probably need 2 rolls per serving, and make 1 or 2 extras. Somebody will eat them! Split the rolls and spread them with margarine or butter. Combine any sort of gameburger (we like mooseburger best) with ½ cup or more finely chopped onion (use sweet onions if available), sea salt, black pepper, dried minced garlic (use sparingly), and Worcestershire Sprinkle. If the Sprinkle is not on hand, use a half teaspoon or so of the sauce instead.

Mix this combination thoroughly and spread on the buttered surfaces of the rolls, building up the edges a bit. Place on a cookie sheet and put under the broiler about 6 inches under the heat source. Broil until the meat is done to your satisfaction. Garnish with raw onion slices. Do not omit this last step, as it seems to be the key to making these rolls really perfect.

To vary, you might sprinkle the rolls with grated cheese the moment they come from under the broiler. Another good variation is to spread the liberally buttered rolls with a mixture of chopped wild fowl (or chicken) livers, dried minced garlic, a few chopped sweet onions, a little chicken soup base, paprika, and pepper to taste. Rabbit liver can be used too, of course, since it tastes almost exactly like chicken liver.

SNACKEROO

It is handy to have something in the fridge from which you can make sandwiches for the lunchboxes. It is also nice to have a good spread for crackers for the after-school crowd. This goes well with a glass of milk.

Pan-fry about 1 pound of moose or caribou liver that has been cut into

51

thick slices. Cook until well done and well browned. Add ½ pound chopped onion. (Usually 1 very large onion will be enough.) Allow the mixture to cool. Grind these together using the finest blade of the food chopper. Season well with salt and pepper and anything else you wish. Hard cook 6 eggs; mash them and add to the meat, mixing well. Next add 1 pint of mayonnaise and again mix thoroughly. The mixture should be moist and of spreading consistency. This recipe makes enough for the usual evening's entertainment, should you care to use it for canapés. In the meantime, keep it in the refrigerator, well covered, for handy snacks.

SPANISH LIVER

Have you ever eaten moose or caribou liver prepared like this? If not, you are in for a treat when you serve this at your table. Of course, calf liver can be fixed this way, too. Incidentally, liver slices more easily if frozen whole and then sliced while still frozen.

Dredge the liver slices in whole wheat flour and brown them in bacon fat or margarine in a frying pan. Sprinkle a little more flour on them and add water enough to not quite cover the slices. Cook until the water is just about all cooked away. Turn the slices and repeat. Then transfer the liver and the "goodie" you scraped from the pan to a casserole with more water. Set the oven to 325°F.

Add the following ingredients in proportions to suit the amount of liver you are cooking: beef soup base; a squirt of tomato paste from the tube; slices of onion; a few garlic cloves, minced; a little chili powder; oregano; black pepper; dried red pepper flakes; and bell pepper pieces. Stir gently to mingle the flavors and put the casserole in the oven, covered. Bake for an hour before testing. If it is nearly tender, leave the cover off for the remainder of the cooking time. If the liquid seems to be cooking away, add a bit more now and then. There should be enough left for some rich gravy.

GAME CASSEROLE

Barbara Sykas uses elk in this recipe; we don't get elk or venison in these parts as often as we do moose or caribou. All are good.

Brown about a pound of mooseburger in 2 tablespoons margarine, crumbling the meat with a fork as it browns. Transfer the meat to a large casserole dish. Cook 1 chopped onion until golden in the fat remaining in the pan. Add more margarine if needed. Shred several good-sized carrots and cook together with other fresh or frozen vegetables of your choice. A total of 4 cups of vegetables is about right. French-cut string beans, corn, peas, celery, or whatever you have on hand will do. No special proportions need be used, but do use lots of carrots. If you wish, add some Potato Buds and 1 can of mushroom pieces to the vegetables after they have been cooked and drained. Stir in seasonings to taste, then add the vegetables to the meat in the casserole. Mix in 1 small can tomato juice and enough hot water to make the mixture juicy but not really wet.

Prepare your favorite corn bread mix according to the directions on the box (I use Texican brand when available), except add about one-quarter to

one-third more milk than it calls for. Drop the batter by spoonfuls on top of the mixture in the casserole. You should have enough batter left to bake a small pan of corn bread. Bake the casserole in a 350°F. oven until the topping is well browned — 20 to 25 minutes, depending on your oven.

– Barbara Sykas

SWEET AND SOUR BLACK BEAR

Bear meat isn't as common in the average household as other big game but, if the bear was young and tender and hadn't learned to catch fish, it should taste good enough for anybody. Be sure that bear meat is thoroughly cooked to avoid trichinosis.

Cube about 2 pounds of bear meat and sprinkle with salt and pepper, then dredge with flour. Brown in a little shortening. After the bear pieces are browned, add ½ cup water, ¼ cup wine vinegar and 2 tablespoons soy sauce. Cover and simmer for an hour or until fork tender. Now add 1 cup of apricot jam and 1 green pepper, diced, and cook 20 minutes or so longer. Serve over hot rice.

ROAST VENISON, GREEK STYLE

This is actually a Greek recipe for lamb, but our friend Peter says he believes it to be even better using venison. Well, try it and see — with either one.

Take about twice the number of potatoes you think will be eaten with the roast; peel and cut up in chunks the size of half a baseball — about 2 inches. Place the peeled potatoes in a glass or stainless steel bowl and marinate with lemon juice — fresh if pos-sible — and a little oregano and pepper. Let the potatoes marinate for 2 hours, turning occasionally so that all are equally marinated.

Place the venison roast in a medium-hot oven. Arrange the potatoes around the meat and roast to your own taste. (Peter likes his medium-rare.) Potatoes will cook a little brown on the outside and should be basted now and then with the leftover marinade.

– Peter W. Sykas

REINDEER POT ROAST

Reindeer is essentially the same as caribou. Some of our Native Eskimos have herds of them which are raised in the Arctic. They have occasional roundups of the animals just as western cowboys do with cattle.

Select a nice 3- to 4-pound reindeer pot roast. Trim off any excess fat. Dredge with flour, coating all sides well. Brown in a Dutch oven, then add salt and pepper to taste, 4 tablespoons minced wild chives, dried or fresh, a liberal handful of dehydrated mixed vegetables, and 2 cups hot water. Cover tightly and allow to cook slowly for 2 hours or more. Check occasionally and add water as needed to maintain the original level. When the reindeer

is tender, add peeled small potatoes, turnips, and carrots. Continue cooking slowly until the vegetables soften. Arrange the meat on a hot platter surrounded by the vegetables. Thicken the liquid with a paste made of whole wheat flour and cold water. Cook the gravy for 8 to 10 minutes. Taste for seasoning and add more if needed.

SEAL CASSEROLE

Whenever you are working with seal meat you had better be sure that all the fat is removed before cooking it. Seal fat is much too rich for most of us.

Select a choice cut of young seal. Cut it into 1- to 2-inch chunks. Dredge in flour seasoned to your taste. Brown the chunks well in margarine or bacon drippings. Place in a casserole and add ½ cup dried wild chives or minced dried onion, 3 whole garlic cloves, a generous dash of thyme, and 1½ cups water (or enough to almost cover the seal chunks). Cook slowly in a 300°F. oven for 1½ to 2 hours. Be sure the meat is tender before removing from the oven.

COOKING WALRUS MEAT

You are not likely to have the opportunity to cook walrus meat, but it is a staple food along our Eskimo coast. An Eskimo friend sent us these cookery tips.

"Walrus is just like other meat, except

they have blubber instead of fat. Fry or boil as you would beef. The blubber tastes odd until you get used to it. The liver is extra good. The tongue is tough, so you had better pickle it."

GAMEBURGER GRAVY

If for some reason you lack a good base for gravy, try this recipe. It will soon prove a family favorite.

Put a little olive oil into a heavy skillet. Crumble any gameburger into the oil, but not too much at a time. Stir it as it browns over medium heat. Keep stirring until the burger is browned nicely. Add a tablespoon or two of flour and stir some more. Now add either milk or water, whichever you prefer, and stir until it bubbles and thickens. You may need to experiment with varying the amounts of burger and flour that you use. Season to taste.

This gravy is delicious served over split hot baking-powder biscuits.

SAUCE'N'BURGER

The germ of the recipe below came from a package of Brownberry Croutons and was adapted to suit our family. You can use asparagus, Brussels sprouts, broccoli, cauliflower, and even steamed cabbage wedges in it.

Prepare cheese sauce by first making a basic White Sauce (p. 91). Enrich it by using part half-and-half instead of all milk for the liquid and add ½ cup grated mild or sharp cheese. Keep the sauce warm in a double boiler while you proceed with the rest of the instructions.

Cook whichever vegetable you

have chosen and arrange it in a serving dish. Crumble raw or cooked gameburger into a skillet that contains 2 or more tablespoons melted margarine. Cook and stir over medium heat until the burger is nicely browned. Scatter the cooked burger over the vegetables in the serving dish. Sauté ½ cup or more Brownberry Onion & Garlic Croutons in the fat left in the skillet. Cook until golden brown. Pour the cheese sauce over the ingredients in the serving dish and sprinkle the sautéed croutons on top.

TRULY DELICIOUS GAMEBURGER CASSEROLE

Any sort of meat can be used with this as long as it is in small pieces. Even fish or fowl will do. Ham is excellent. If you get a chance at some of the extra-sweet onions such as the Georgia Sweets, do try this dish. If you don't use sweet onions, you had better cut down on the amount you use, as the more powerful onions would be too strong in such quantity.

Select one or more good-sized potatoes for each person to be served and the same number of sweet onions. Crumble a pound or more of any burger into a small amount of margarine melted in a large frying pan; brown well, stirring the meat as it browns. Pare the potatoes and peel and slice the onions. Butter a good-sized baking dish or casserole.

Slice a layer of potatoes into the dish. Cover with onion slices and then a layer of the browned meat. Then repeat the process until all of your potatoes, onions, and meat are used. Prepare a sauce, using 2 tablespoons margarine blended with 1 tablespoon flour per person. Add 1 cup milk per person and cook over low heat until the sauce is thickened. Season the sauce as you please while it is cooking with salt, pepper, and various herbs. You may need to add more milk to create a pourable consistency — thick, but not too thick. Pour this sauce over the contents of the casserole; set in a preheated 350°F. oven and bake for 1½ hours, or until the potatoes are soft.

ALASKA MINCEMEAT

This is another one of those recipes where you can let your imagination run wild. Use any kind of big game burger or a combination of 2 or more kinds.

Stir together in a large preserving kettle the following ingredients: 2½ to 3 pounds gameburger, 4 cups liquid (apple cider, meat stock, fruit juice, or a combination of these), 1 cup apricot or other preserves, 1 cup dried currants, 1 pound golden raisins, 3 cups soaked dried apples, 1 cup molasses, 1 cup white sugar, 1 cup light brown sugar, 1 pound ground suet, 2 tablespoons lemon juice, 1 cup candied lemon peel, 2 tablespoons dried lemon peel, 2 tablespoons dried orange peel, 1 tablespoon rum flavoring, and 1 tablespoon brandy flavoring.

If all these ingredients are not on hand, make substitutions where necessary. Stir to mingle well and cook. Bring to a boil and then reduce the heat to simmer. Cook gently for an hour or more. The mincemeat should gradually thicken. It will thicken even more as it cools.

Cool and pour into square 1-quart plastic freezer containers. Wait until the mincemeat is completely cold before putting it in the freezer. This kind of mincemeat may be used "as is" or

diluted with fresh or dried apples or other fruit before you use it in your holiday pies.

MINCEMEAT DROP COOKIES

These cookies are moist and will keep fine, provided the cookie jar is hidden well.

Cream ¾ cup shortening and 1½ cups sugar together in a bowl. Add 3 well-beaten eggs and beat until light. Sift 3 cups flour with 1 teaspoon baking soda and ¾ teaspoon salt (or less). Add half of the flour mixture to the creamed mixture. Then stir in finely crumbled mincemeat and 3 tablespoons water. Add 1 cup nut meats, chopped, and the remaining flour mixture. Stir until well blended. Drop from a teaspoon onto a greased baking sheet. Bake at 350°F. for 10 to 15 minutes. Makes about 4 dozen.

– Mary Taylor

LAYERED GAME CASSEROLE

Here is a well-balanced one-dish meal in itself — all but the dessert. This is a recipe where you can make all sorts of substitutions, as you can readily see. It is a good one to experiment with.

In the bottom of a large baking dish, spread a cup or more of cooked rice. Add a layer of greens (dandelion, nettle, young fireweed, or other young and tender native greens); sprinkle with any seasonings you choose. Now pour over this an 8-ounce can of tomato sauce (mixed with ½ can of water) and ½ cup each wild chives (snipped) and strips of green bell pepper. Finish off with a thick layer (about 1½ pounds) of gameburger such as venison, mountain sheep, or other big game. Sprinkle with salt and pepper and more chopped wild chives. Pour another can of tomato sauce combined with water over the lot. Top with several strips of bacon. Cover and bake for an hour or more in a 350°F. oven. Remove the cover and bake for another 30 minutes.

COUNTRY-STYLE MEAT PIE

Here is another recipe that will allow your imagination to roam. Any big game is suitable for the meat. So is small game, for that matter.

Have ready a heavy-duty pan with a little oil heating in it. Flour 1-inch chunks of the meat well and place in the pan. Don't crowd the meat or it won't brown properly. You may need to use 2 pans or use the same pan twice, depending on the amount of meat you are cooking. Turn the meat so that all sides are well browned. Cover with water and cook. (This is really a stew with a crust.) Add potato pieces, onion slices, carrots, a little tomato paste, beef soup base, and anything else you like. A few green peas will give the pie a visual appeal. Cook until the meat and vegetables are tender. Thicken the gravy with a paste made from cold water and flour. Transfer the stew to a deep casserole dish. Use your favorite biscuit mix to make baking-powder biscuits. Roll out and cut the biscuits. Place on top of the stew in the casserole dish and bake in a preheated 400°F. oven until the biscuits are done. You'll probably need to bake extra biscuits.

As a variation you can make dumplings with the stew instead of making it into a meat pie. Follow the directions for dumplings on the biscuit mix package.

MEAT LOAF MIX-UP

Meat loaf is one of those dishes that can be varied almost endlessly. Try being creative with it and see what you can come up with (not too creative, though).

Soak a slice or two of whole wheat bread in a little milk in a bowl. When it is thoroughly moistened, crumble into it about 1½ pounds of any good gameburger that is not too fat. Break up the bread well as you stir in the burger. Season with whatever you wish, but be sure to use a little beef soup base (and not too much salt). Thyme, pepper, marjoram, vegetable seasoning, garlic powder, and dried minced onions are all good, and so are many others. Break an egg into the bowl and stir it in along with a small can of creamed corn, half a can of mushroom soup, or whatever you like. As we said in the beginning, be creative. Put the mixture in a loaf pan or shape and place on a baking sheet.

Bake in a preheated 350°F. oven for about an hour. This may be served with hot tomato sauce or other gravy, or it is good cold and sliced and made into sandwiches.

FEATHERS AND FUR:
Game Birds and Rabbits

Our wild fowl population varies greatly with the seasons, for Alaska is on the great migration routes for waterfowl. The upland birds, such as grouse and ptarmigan, are more nearly permanent residents. Rabbits (or hare) fluctuate in numbers from year to year as they are cyclic. Some years they are in great abundance and then — CRASH — they are all gone, only to build up again gradually over a period of several years. Then we again have quantities of them in the freezer.

SPRUCE CHICKEN JUNIPER

Spruce chickens may also be disjointed and fried as you would chicken, but the parts are so small they are then more suited to being served as hors d'oeuvres.

Dry-pluck several spruce chickens and wipe the body cavities clean and dry. Fasten a thin slice of bacon around each bird with a toothpick. Fry them in butter or margarine in a heavy skillet over medium-high heat. Turn the birds at frequent intervals until they are a healthy brown. Meanwhile prepare the juniper mixture.

Crush from 10 to 20 ripe juniper berries and add 1 cup of boiling water, a little black pepper, and some chicken soup base, with enough minced dried onion to flavor the birds a little.

Pour this mixture over the fowls, cover the skillet, and let them simmer slowly for an hour or more. When the birds are tender pour a cup of sweet or sour cream or evaporated milk over them and continue to simmer gently for another 20 minutes or so. Taste the sauce and add more seasoning if you wish. Serve with big Matanuska baked potatoes.

MARINATED SPRUCE GROUSE

The following method of marinating is unusual to say the least but it is effective as well. You will need at least 6 grouse.

Cut the grouse down one side of the backbone. Flatten the fowl a little with pressure from the palm of your hand. Using a very sharp boning knife remove the backbone and ribs. Put the birds in a bowl and cover with 2 cups of half-and-half. Set aside for at least an hour. Combine ½ cup

whole wheat flour, ½ teaspoon salt, ¼ teaspoon black pepper, a good pinch of nutmeg, ¼ teaspoon ground cloves, ¼ teaspoon dried thyme leaves, and 4 or 5 well-crushed juniper berries.

Remove the grouse from the marinade and roll them in the flour mixture, shaking off any excess. Heat ¼ cup of a good grade of olive oil in a large, heavy skillet and sauté the grouse until browned on both sides and cooked through — about 30 minutes or slightly less. While the birds are cooking, prepare the following sauce and toast 6 slices of bread. Spread the toast with wild Currant Jelly (p. 69) and place the cooked grouse on top.

SAUCE

Melt 2 tablespoons margarine in a heavy saucepan and stir in 2 tablespoons flour. Let cook slowly for 2 or 3 minutes and then gradually add 1 cup of milk. Stir over low heat until the sauce is thickened. Add 2 tablespoons Madeira wine and a little salt and pepper. Pour the sauce over the grouse and serve hot.

MULLIGATAWNY SOUP

Mulligatawny just comes naturally once you have removed the breasts of wild fowl for braising. There is little meat left after the breasts are taken off, but what little there is won't be wasted if you use it this way. Use the gizzards, hearts, and livers, too.

Be sure the fowl pieces are all clean. Put them in a sizeable kettle with plenty of water to more than cover. Add 2 or 3 teaspoons curry powder and 1 large onion, chopped. Cook until the meat is tender. Remove the fowl pieces from the broth, pick the meat

off the bones, and return it to the broth. Add enough water to make about 8 cups total. Add also 1¼ cups rice (brown rice if available), ½ cup lentils, ½ cup green split peas, a handful of dried red and green bell pepper pieces, and a small can of mushroom stems and pieces. For seasoning you may want to use sea salt, a little chicken soup base, black pepper, celery flakes, and a few others. Now (and this is what makes mulligatawny a different kind of soup) add at this point ½ cup diced dried apples. Cook until the rice and apples are tender. Just before removing from the heat add 1½ cups half-and-half. This soup is almost a meal in itself.

WILD GOOSE IN MUSHROOM SAUCE

Wild ducks and rabbits can be prepared this way, too; just cut them into serving-size pieces. Use bacon fat for browning, if available.

Cut the bird in quarters or smaller. Brown the pieces in a Dutch oven in bacon fat or olive oil. When the parts are nicely browned, add mushroom soup (a can or two, depending on the amount of the fowl), diluted with a little water. Add sliced onion to taste and chervil, thyme, marjoram, chicken soup base, pepper, and a clove of garlic, minced. Cover and simmer over low heat until the meat is tender. This last part of the cooking may be done in the oven if you wish.

ROAST WILD GOOSE

Wild goose makes a good Christmas dinner and it is usually tender enough, unless you have bagged an old-timer — in which case you had better marinate it.

An especially good recipe for all-purpose marinade can be found in the Tail Ends chapter (p. 92).

Clean the goose as needed and wipe out the inside with paper towels. Rub a little salt on the inside, too. Use the recipe for stuffing to be found in the Tail Ends chapter (p. 91), or simply put in a couple of peeled and cored apples or the leaves from several stalks of celery. Place the stuffed bird in a roasting pan, breast-side up. Rub a little margarine over the breast or lay several strips of bacon across it, as geese tend to be dry at times. Roast in a 325°F. oven, basting with pan juices occasionally. After an hour and a half, begin testing for doneness by squeezing the thigh with a folded paper towel. If it yields easily to pressure it is done.

Stir a little flour into the pan juices after you have removed the fowl to a heated platter. Add water, a little at a time, until you have gravy just thick enough to suit you. Serve with lowbush cranberry relish.

DUCK STEW WITH DUMPLINGS

Wild ducks lend themselves well to stew. They sometimes need quite long cooking because of their age, and perhaps that is why they are so well adapted to this dish.

Cut 2 ducks in half lengthwise and place in a large kettle. Cut 3 medium onions into chunks and slice 4 or 5 medium-size carrots into the pot. Cover the duck and vegetables with water and season to taste with salt, pepper, a smidgen of curry, thyme, and any other seasonings you like. Bring to a boil; then reduce heat and simmer for 1½ to 2 hours, or until the

birds are tender. Thicken the liquid for gravy with a paste of flour and cold water. Remove the meat and keep it warm while you make the dumplings. Using Bisquick, Krusteaz, or any similar biscuit mix, follow the directions for making dumplings. Add 1 teaspoon dried parsley to the dough and bits of sharp cheese. Serve the fowl pieces on a large platter with dumplings piled around the edge. The vegetables can remain in the gravy.

BARBECUED WILD DUCK

Wild fowl can be pretty tough at times and sometimes they don't have the best of flavors. Soaking in salt water or vinegar water will remedy this.

Soak the ducks you plan to cook in salted water overnight. Dry them with paper towels and split them open. Dredge them in whole wheat flour to which a little salt has been added. Brown the split ducks in 1 cup melted margarine, then place them in a roasting pan. Add half a cup of hot water; cover and bake in a 325°F. oven until tender. It will take about 3 hours to roast the ducks, so you will need to add more hot water to keep the birds from drying out. During the last 45 minutes, baste with a sauce made from the margarine left in the browning pan, to which is added 1 cup chili sauce, 1 teaspoon Tabasco sauce, 2 teaspoons paprika, 3 tablespoons wine vinegar, and 2 tablespoons Worcestershire sauce. Taste after mix-

ing to test the seasoning and correct it if necessary. Baste several times during this last 45 minutes and leave the cover off the roasting pan. Serve any remaining sauce with the barbecued duck at the table.

DUCK SURPRISE

Sometimes it is difficult to know just what to do with the ducks one has bagged. If you keep this recipe in mind you will have no trouble deciding how to prepare them.

Simmer together for 10 minutes the following combination: 1 cup salad oil; ½ cup vinegar; ¼ cup soy sauce; 6 cloves garlic, crushed; 1 sprig rosemary; 1 tablespoon celery seeds; and salt and pepper to taste. Cut your ducks in half and baste with the mixture. Grill over an open flame. Bake some potatoes to go with these and toss a green salad. Sourdough French Bread (p. 85) is mighty good with it, too.   – Hank Rosenthal

DUCK CASSEROLE

You can't go wrong on this one because it is so easy. Cook the ducks in any style you choose — they can even be left over from a dinner. Allow them to cool and then go ahead.

In a greased shallow casserole dish, arrange in layers: two-thirds of a package Pepperidge Farm Corn Bread Stuffing crumbs; 1 package frozen French-cut string beans, partly cooked; 2 or 3 tablespoons blanched slivered almonds (optional); and the duck meat cut into small chunks. Make a White Sauce using the recipe on p. 91. Enrich the recipe by using half-and-half or part heavy cream in

place of the milk; also add various additional seasonings such as thyme, red pepper flakes, or a small amount of curry powder. Pour this sauce over the contents of the casserole. Moisten 1 cup Corn Bread Stuffing crumbs with ¼ cup hot water and 2 tablespoons melted butter. Spread the moistened crumbs over the casserole as a topping. Bake in a preheated 400°F. oven for about 30 minutes.

BRAISED GROUSE BREASTS

There isn't much to a spruce grouse but breast, so this is the recipe we use most often. (Sometimes we roast them as we would a small chicken.) After the breasts are removed, save the rest of the grouse for soup. Let's hope your grouse were winged before they started eating the spruce. Wild ducks and ptarmigan are delicious prepared this way, too.

Remove the breasts from several spruce grouse; dredge with whole wheat flour and brown on each side in a little melted fat. Add ½ cup or more of water together with a level teaspoon of chicken soup base. If you have reason to believe that the birds are old and tough, use tomato juice instead of water or part water and part tomato juice. Cover the pan tightly and allow to simmer slowly until the fowl is tender. More liquid will be needed from time to time, and seasonings such as onion, thyme, curry, and others may be used. A can of mushroom stems and pieces is good in this. Instead of simmering on top of the stove, this may be cooked in the oven. When the breasts are fork tender they are done. Thicken the gravy with a flour and cold water paste and serve over hot baking-powder biscuits.

BAKED GROUSE OR PTARMIGAN

Alaskan cooks can argue forever about the merits of skinning or not skinning wild fowl. As you see, this one is a "skinner." So far as we can tell, it doesn't make all that much difference.

Skin the birds and clean inside just as you would a chicken. Prepare a good dressing and stuff the birds full. Corn Bread Stuffing is our choice (p. 91). Lay 2 strips of hickory-smoked bacon across the breast of each grouse and wrap each loosely but airtight in aluminum foil. Place in a roasting pan and bake for 80 minutes in a preheated 350°F. oven. Open the foil on one of the birds to see if the fat from the bacon has cooked down into the breast as it should. If it has, open the foil wide on all the birds and allow them to bake uncovered for another 15 to 20 minutes to brown a bit.

CREAMED WILD FOWL

Use the basic White Sauce recipe (p. 91) and go on from there. You will want to use a lot of seasoning in this recipe.

Leftover stir-fried ptarmigan (or other wild fowl or almost any other cooked meat) will work in this versatile recipe. Cut the meat into bite-size pieces and put it into the reheating White Sauce (p. 91). Add a little chicken soup base or other soup base, depending on the kind of meat you are using. Some snipped wild chives or sliced green onions are good, but best of all is a few slices of sweet onion previously stir-fried with a like amount of sweet bell pepper bits. Lacking any of these, you can use minced dehydrated onions and dried

bell pepper pieces. They should be cooked together in a little water for 15 minutes or so before adding to the main dish.

For seasoning, add some thyme, marjoram, either chervil or parsley, a little paprika, and other herbs and spices of your choice. You can also stir in some extra margarine for flavor. Taste-test and correct the seasoning to your satisfaction. Serve over hot biscuits or toast points.

WILD BIRD CASSEROLE

The original recipe calls for chicken, but it works equally well with spruce grouse, ptarmigan, ducks, and geese.

Spread the contents of 1 small box of Minute Rice (uncooked) on the bottom of a 9x13-inch baking dish. Sprinkle this with half a package of dry onion soup mix. Mix together 1 can cream of mushroom soup, 1 can cream of celery soup, and 1 cup half-and-half. Pour most of this mixture over the rice. Place the cut-up pieces of wild fowl on top of this. Sprinkle with the rest of the package of onion soup mix and pour on the rest of the soup/cream mixture. Cover with foil and bake at 325°F. for 2 hours. You should not need to add any salt or other seasonings.

PTARMIGAN STIR-FRY

Spruce hen, rabbit, or even chicken can be used in this recipe, but be sure they are young and tender. We think ptarmigan is best. If you have any of this left over, it is fine for the lunch box, for snacks, or creamed on toast.

Get out your largest skillet and put into it a tablespoon of margarine on

low heat. As it melts prepare the various ingredients. The pieces of fowl should be small and boneless. We like a few slices of sweet onion, several pieces of snipped wild chives, a few narrow strips of red or green sweet bell pepper (or both) cut in 1-inch pieces, and a very few puffballs, sliced. Use also a slice or two of lemon cut in quarters or a couple of squirts from the homestead lemon. Also prepare (and this is what really makes the dish) a couple of thin slices of crystallized ginger, cut into slivers.

Pour all the ingredients into the skillet and set the heat at medium-high. Use a pancake turner turned over to keep stirring and pushing the food around in the skillet. Add a little chicken soup base for extra flavor, too. You may need to add more margarine to the pan. Two or 3 cherry tomatoes cut in quarters can be used, though we often do without them. Sprinkle on a bit of paprika and salt, but no pepper. Flip the pan ingredients over occasionally and keep stirring. The onions should be golden, but the peppers will still be crisp when they are ready to eat. Cut into a piece of the meat to see if it is done. It should cut easily with a fork. Serve with fresh Sourdough French Bread (p.85) if you have it — or with whole wheat bread if you don't.

WILD FOWL SOUP

Most people who have wild fowl to cook use the breasts for braising or stewing. There is no need to discard the rest of the bird. Make a delectable soup from the thighs, drumsticks, backs, and wings of any wild fowl. Of course, you can use the breasts in the soup, too.

Boil the carcass of a duck, grouse, or ptarmigan until the meat is soft enough to fall off the bones. With a slotted spoon remove the meat and bones from the broth and allow to cool. When cool enough to handle, separate the meat from the bones and discard the bones and any skin. Return the meat to the broth, cutting any large pieces into smaller bits. Simmer gently. Add a hefty dollop of chicken soup base and any other seasonings that you like. We usually add either whole wheat noodles or rice; either one can be incorporated at this point. The soup should bubble gently for half an hour or so for the seasonings to be properly mingled with the other ingredients. Either croutons or crackers go well with this soup.

BRUNSWICK STEW

Old, tired chickens were used in Virginia, where my mother's family came from, to make this dish. Mom converted it into a recipe for domestic rabbits, and we now use it for wild rabbits and elderly geese.

Divide the rabbit or goose into serving-size pieces. In a large pan cover the pieces with boiling water, then cover the pan. Allow to simmer for an hour. Add 2 teaspoons salt, cover again, and continue cooking slowly until the meat is tender. Take out the pieces of meat with a slotted spoon. Remove the bones and cut the meat into 1-inch (or smaller) pieces. Put the meat back in the pan and add 3 tomatoes, cut in quarters, or a can of condensed tomato soup. Slice 2 small onions thinly and stir in along with 3 medium potatoes, cut in small chunks, and a cup of green lima beans. Add 1 tablespoon brown sugar and 1 tablespoon chicken soup base. Cook until the beans and potatoes are

tender. Then add a cup of whole-kernel corn and 6 tablespoons margarine. Cook another 10 minutes and it is ready to serve.

OVEN-FRIED RABBIT

Since rabbit tastes so much like fowl, we often use the recipes interchangeably. The original recipe calls for chicken, but several other kinds of meat, including veal, may be used instead.

After the rabbits have been dressed, cut them into serving-size pieces and put them in a single layer on a cookie sheet. Salt and pepper each piece and put a dab of margarine or butter on each. Then sprinkle paprika generously over them all. They should be absolutely covered with paprika. Place the pan on the upper shelf of a preheated 375°F. oven and bake for 20 minutes. Remove the pan from the oven. Turn the pieces of rabbit and repeat the seasoning, again using lots of paprika. Return to the oven for about 10 to 15 minutes. With the point of a sharp knife test one of the leg pieces (leg pieces will probably be the toughest) to see if the rabbit is done. If not, you can place under the broiler for not more than 5 minutes if you wish.

Put the rabbit pieces on a heated platter and keep warm. Scrape the drippings into a saucepan. Stir in a tablespoon or two of flour, and when the flour is absorbed add milk — about 1½ cups at first. Stir constantly with the pan over medium heat. When the gravy thickens, you can tell whether you need more milk or not. It all depends on how thick you like your gravy. This kind of gravy is great on mashed potatoes.

SMOTHERED RABBIT

For this recipe be sure the rabbit is a youngster. An older one will taste all right, but will take considerably longer to cook.

Cut the rabbit into serving-size pieces and dredge with whole wheat flour. Place the pieces in a heavy skillet that contains ⅛ inch oil and is over medium heat. Cook the pieces until they are brown on one side. While browning, sprinkle with paprika, thyme, and pepper. Turn the pieces and season the other side. When both sides have browned well, sprinkle with flour and add a small amount of water. Cover and reduce the heat to simmer. When the liquid is almost all cooked away, turn the pieces and again sprinkle with flour and add a little water. Repeat this process 4 or 5 times. When the meat is tender, remove the pieces to a heated serving dish. Scrape the particles loose that stick to the bottom of the pan. Add 1 tablespoon chicken soup base and 2 cups milk. While this is coming to a boil mix whole wheat flour and cold water to a thin paste. Pour the paste gradually into the boiling milk and cook and stir for 10 minutes. If the gravy is not thick enough to suit your taste, just add a little more of the flour-water paste and cook some more. Serve with mashed potatoes and a tossed green salad.

IT'S THE BERRIES:
Wild Berries and Rose Hips

All of our wild fruits have much vitamin C in their makeup, but the fruit of the wild rose has the most. The farther north the rose hips are harvested the richer in that essential vitamin they are. The lowbush cranberry, found throughout the state, is a most accommodating fruit, for it is useful in many ways. Several species of blueberries make their home in Alaska, and they are quite widespread. We use other varieties of native wild berries, too, when they are available.

BLUEBERRY MUFFINS

Blueberry muffins are one of our favorite breakfast foods in late summer. Lowbush cranberries are good in muffins, too, but they require a lot more sugar.

Sift a scant 2 cups all-purpose flour into a mixing bowl, reserving ¼ cup for later use. Sift with the flour 3 teaspoons baking powder, ½ teaspoon salt, and 4 tablespoons sugar. In another bowl mix 2 slightly beaten eggs, 1 cup milk, and ¼ cup melted butter or margarine. Pour this over the flour mixture. Stir just enough to moisten the flour. The batter should not be smooth. Dust 1 cup fresh blueberries with the reserved flour and stir gently into the batter. Pour paper muffin cup liners two-thirds full of the batter and bake about 15 minutes in a preheated 400°F. oven.

BLUEBERRY SALAD

Fruit salads are especially welcome in the warmer days of summer, and that is when the blueberries are available, too.

Prepare lemon Jello according to the directions on the box, adding a dash of ginger. When the Jello begins to thicken, add raw wild blueberries that have been cleaned and sorted. They may be either fresh or frozen. If frozen, allow them to dry for an hour or so before using, to get rid of excess moisture.

When the Jello is firm, spoon portions onto crisp lettuce leaves and serve with a fruit salad dressing. One good dressing is mayonnaise diluted with fruit juice. Garnish the individual salads with a few perfect berries.

BLUEBERRY GINGER CRISP

Canned and drained blueberries can be used for this dessert, but if you can get the wild ones right off the bushes the crisp will taste much better.

Using a rolling pin, finely crush about 16 gingersnaps placed inside a sealed plastic bag. In a small saucepan melt ¼ cup butter or margarine; remove from the heat. Blend in the gingersnap crumbs, ¼ cup chopped nuts (more if you wish), 2 tablespoons brown sugar, and a few drops of lemon juice. Arrange 2 to 3 cups blueberries in a buttered shallow 2-quart baking dish. Sprinkle the crumb mixture over the fruit. Bake in a 350°F. oven for 25 to 30 minutes. Serve while warm, with or without half-and-half.

BLUEBERRY CUSTARD

The custard sauce described here is an excellent accompaniment to blueberries. It can be used with other fruit, but somehow it seems to suit blueberries best.

In a large saucepan blend together 4 large eggs, slightly beaten, ½ cup sugar, and ¼ teaspoon salt. Gradually stir in 2½ cups milk. Cook, stirring constantly, until the mixture thickens and will coat a metal spoon. Stir in 2 teaspoons vanilla. Cool rapidly by setting the saucepan in a bowl of ice or ice-cold water and stirring for a few minutes. When the custard is cold, cover closely and refrigerate to chill thoroughly. To serve, spoon fresh blueberries into dessert dishes and pour a generous helping of the custard over them.

If you use lowbush cranberries or other very sour berries, crush them first and then mix in a little sugar before pouring on the sauce.

BLUEBERRY PARFAIT

This beautiful dessert tastes as good as it looks and is easy enough to prepare, but it does take a little time. Be sure to save out a few nice, big, perfect blueberries to use on top of the finished product.

Combine 2 cups blueberries and ½ cup sugar and cook slowly until syrupy — about 5 minutes. Chill. Dissolve 1 small package strawberry gelatin in 1 cup boiling water and then add 1 cup of cold water. Chill the gelatin until it begins to thicken. Fold half of the berry mixture into half of the gelatin and pour into parfait glasses. Chill until firm. Chill the remaining gelatin until firm and then beat until fluffy. Fold in the rest of the fruit mixture. Whip 1 cup whipping cream until it holds peaks, then fold it into the gelatin-fruit mixture, together with ½ cup finely chopped walnuts or pecans. Pour this mixture over the layer already in the parfait glasses. Put about 3 perfect berries on top of each serving and chill the parfaits until firm and ready to serve.

POP-IN-A-PAN PIES

With this recipe, you can make enough filling for four 9-inch pies. The fillings can be stored for 6 months or so. In good harvest years we always had enough blueberries for this.

Wash and drain 4 quarts fresh blueberries, then mix well with 3½ cups sugar, ¾ cup quick tapioca, 6 tablespoons lemon juice, and 1 teaspoon salt. Line four 9-inch pie pans with heavy-duty aluminum foil. Allow the foil to extend 4 or 5 inches beyond the rim of each pan. Pour the filling equally into the foil-lined pans. Fold the foil loosely over the tops and

freeze until solid. Remove the frozen filling from the pans, fold the foil tightly, and return the fillings to the freezer.

To bake one of the pies, prepare pastry for a double-crust pie and line a 9-inch pie pan with a bottom crust. Take a filling from the freezer and peel the foil off quickly. Do not let the filling thaw. Pop it into the pastry-lined pan while still frozen and dot with small dabs of margarine. Add the top crust and slit vents. Bake in a preheated 425°F. oven until the syrup boils up with heavy bubbles. Be sure to place a large piece of aluminum foil on the bottom shelf of the oven to catch any overflow.

DOUBLE-ZIP BLUEBERRY PIE

You will need one baked pie shell for this unusual blueberry pie. Perhaps you had better make two of them, because calls for second helpings will be certain.

Combine 1 cup sugar, 3 tablespoons cornstarch, and ½ teaspoon salt in a saucepan. Add ½ cup water and 2 cups blueberries. Cook until the mixture is thick and clear, stirring all the while. Remove from the heat and stir in 1 tablespoon butter or margarine and a couple of squirts from your homestead lemon. Cool. Mix 2 more cups of raw blueberries into the cooked mixture and pour the lot into the pie shell (or shells). Heap with whipped cream before serving.

BLUEBERRY PIE

Blueberry pie is almost as much of an institution as apple pie in our country. And we have several species of berries to choose from. The ones that grow in the alpine areas seem to be larger and sweeter, but maybe that is pure imagination.

Make up a batch of pie crust from your favorite mix. (We use Betty Crocker's Pie Crust sticks or Krusteaz. The sticks are less labor.) Line a 9-inch pie pan with pastry. Sprinkle a light dusting of flour on the bottom of the crust in the pan. In a small bowl mix together 2 cups cleaned blueberries, 1 cup sugar, a dash of lemon juice, and a few grains of nutmeg. Sprinkle the mixture with a little flour and mix again gently so as not to break the berries. Pour into a saucepan and cook slowly for a few minutes — bring just to the boil, then remove from the heat. Meanwhile, put 1 cup of raw blueberries in the prepared pie crust. After the cooked berries have cooled a little, pour them over the raw ones in the crust. Put the top crust in place and slit vents in it so that steam can escape.

Place the pie in a preheated 425°F. oven for 10 minutes. Reduce the heat to 350°F. and continue baking until the crust is well browned. To help in keeping your oven clean, put a cookie sheet or a large sheet of heavy-duty aluminum foil on the shelf below the pie. Such an arrangement will catch any drips, and there will probably be plenty of them.

BERRY-BANANA NUGGETS

Nuggets are useful in taking care of those overripe bananas that no one wants to eat. The recipe also gives you a good method for using only a few blueberries. Lowbush cranberries are successful here, too, but they demand more sugar.

Dredge 1 cup firm blueberries in ¼ cup flour and set aside. Sift and mix

1¾ cups flour, 1 teaspoon baking soda, and ½ teaspoon salt and set aside. Cream 1 stick of room-temperature margarine until light and fluffy, and gradually stir in 1 cup sugar. Add 2 slightly beaten eggs, 1 cup mashed ripe banana, and 1 tablespoon grated orange rind. In a separate container combine ¼ cup milk, 1 teaspoon vanilla, and ½ teaspoon almond extract.

Add the dry ingredients and the milk mixture alternately to the bananas, beginning and ending with the dry ones. Blend well after each addition. Stir in 1 cup shredded coconut and ½ cup chopped nuts. Add the berries and stir gently to avoid breaking their skins. Preheat the oven to 350°F. Fill paper-lined muffin cups only one-quarter full. Bake about 25 minutes, or until the surface of the nuggets is well browned and springs back when touched with a fingertip.

BLUEBERRY OMELET

Have you ever tried using berries in an omelet? Now is your chance to make a unique dessert.

With a fork mix 2 eggs, 2 tablespoons water, ¼ teaspoon salt, and a shake of pepper. Heat 1 tablespoon butter or margarine in an 8-inch frying pan or omelet pan over medium heat. Heat until the butter is just hot enough to sizzle when a drop of water is splashed into it. Pour in the egg mixture. This will set at the edges at once. With a pancake turner that is turned over, carefully push the cooked portions at the edges toward the center so that the uncooked portions flow to the bottom of the pan. Tilt the pan as necessary so the uncooked eggs can flow. Slide the pan rapidly back and forth over the heat to keep the mixture in motion and sliding freely.

While the top is still moist and creamy-looking, drop on some warmed blueberries. With the pancake turner, fold in half or roll the omelet, turning it out onto a plate with a quick flip of the wrist. Sprinkle the omelet with powdered sugar. Serves one.

ALASKAN PARTY CHEESECAKES

Here is the ever-popular cheesecake in a simple form. This recipe will make up to 36 miniature cheesecakes, but can easily be cut down to a third that size.

Beat until creamy three 8-ounce packages cream cheese (at room temperature), 3 eggs, ¾ cup sugar, and 1 teaspoon vanilla. Line cupcake pans with paper liners. Place a vanilla wafer in each liner. Pour in the cheese mixture to make the liners one-half to two-thirds full, depending on the amount of fruit topping desired. Bake at 400°F. for 15 to 20 minutes. Prepare the fruit filling while the little cakes are baking and pour it onto the cakes while they are still hot. Cool the cheesecakes and freeze. Remove the cakes from the freezer a couple of hours before serving and peel off the papers while the cakes are still frozen.

FRUIT FILLING

Heat 4 cups of wild blueberries or raspberries in a pan, together with 1 tablespoon lemon juice, 2 tablespoons butter or margarine, ⅓ cup flour, ½ cup sugar and ½ teaspoon cinnamon if desired. Cook until the mixture thickens. Canned fruit fillings may be substituted if fresh berries are unavailable.
– *Kitty Evans*

CURRANT JELLY

Wild Currant Jelly is an excellent accompaniment to any big game and to other meat as well.

Clean the currants, but do not wash them unless really necessary. Don't bother to remove the stems. Cook enough of them to make about 4 cups of juice. Use only enough water to get the juice flowing and simmer slowly until the fruit is soft, stirring occasionally. Crush the currants and strain them through a damp jelly bag. Don't squeeze the bag, or the jelly will be cloudy instead of clear. Return the juice to the pan after the fruit has strained for several hours or overnight. Bring quickly to a boil and boil for 3 minutes or so. Add 3 cups of sugar for 4 cups of juice and stir until all the sugar is dissolved. Bring to a boil again. After 3 minutes test the mixture to see if it has reached the jelly stage (see below); repeat every 3 minutes until the jelly stage has been reached. When cooked enough, remove the jelly from the heat and skim off the foam. Pour the jelly into hot sterilized jelly glasses and seal with paraffin.

To test for the jelly stage, dip a cold metal spoon into the boiling jelly and then hold it about 18 inches above the pan. Turn the spoon so that the liquid runs off the edge. The jelly stage has been reached when more than 2 drops form and run together before falling from the edge of the spoon.

CURRANT SAUCE

A tart sauce sometimes seems just right with wild game, and this one should fit the bill. It is superb with grilled or roasted venison, moose, or caribou.

Cut the rind of an orange into tiny slivers about the size of spruce needles — a tedious job, but worth it for the result. Cook these slivers with 1 cup of Madeira wine (or port), simmering gently until the volume is reduced by two-thirds. Now add the juice of the orange, 2 tablespoons of lemon juice, a dash of ground ginger, and ½ to ¾ cup wild Currant Jelly. Continue to simmer until the jelly is melted.

CURRANT JELLY SAUCE

This is a super sauce to serve with any game but it's especially delicious with venison, caribou, and the like.

Melt 2 tablespoons bacon drippings or margarine and cook slowly until the fat is well browned but not blackened. Add 2 tablespoons flour, a dash of pepper, and ½ teaspoon salt. Then gradually add 1 cup of Game Stock (p.34) or stock made with beef soup base and water. Boil for 2 minutes. Melt ¼ to ½ cup Currant Jelly in the sauce and season further with either sherry or port wine.

CRANBERRY PUNCH

Lowbush cranberry juice is excellent for all sorts of recipes. Among other things it makes a good base for a most refreshing beverage that is fine to serve at parties, receptions, and the like.

Adjust the proportions in this recipe to suit your own taste. The way it is given here is the way we like it at our house. We will assume that you have already stashed away in the freezer, or some other cool place, the fruit juices mentioned here. If not, you are out of luck until next season.

Put a plentiful supply of ice cubes in a large punch bowl. Pour over the ice 2 quarts of pure lowbush cranberry juice and 3 quarts of wild raspberry juice. If you have some rose hip juice or syrup, add a couple of cups to the fruit juices in the bowl. Add also your favorite sparkling water in any amount you wish and then stir in about 1 cup of pure honey. Stir just enough to mix well. Add more ice from time to time if it needs it. You can also add some orange juice if you like. For hot days in summer keep a pitcherful of this punch in the fridge. You don't really have to make this large a quantity.

CRANBERRY BREAD

This basic cranberry bread recipe came to us from the Extension Service, but it has been embellished freely and can easily take the place of the traditional fruitcake at holiday time. It freezes well and is also a good shipper.

Bring to a boil the juice of 2 oranges with enough water added to make 1¾ cups liquid. Add 6 tablespoons margarine and 2 tablespoons grated orange rind. Set aside to cool. Sift 4 cups flour, reserving ¼ cup for later use. Sift the flour again with 1 teaspoon salt, 1 teaspoon baking soda, 1½ teaspoons baking powder, 2 cups sugar, 1 teaspoon each nutmeg and cinnamon, and ½ teaspoon each cloves, allspice, and ginger. Transfer the sifted ingredients to a large bowl and make a well in the center. Pour the cooled liquid into the well and stir just enough to moisten. Add 2 well-beaten eggs and stir gently.

Sprinkle the reserved flour over 3 cups clean, dry lowbush cranberries on a flat surface (a cookie sheet is great for this). Now add to the batter the floured fruit and 2 cups coarsely chopped walnuts and stir carefully to keep from breaking the berries.

Line loaf pans with strips of aluminum foil. Spoon enough dough into the lined pans so that they will be slightly more than half full. Preheat the oven to 350°F. Bake the loaves from 45 minutes to 1½ hours; the time depends on the size of the loaves. Allow the baked bread to stand on racks for 20 minutes or so, then remove from the pans and peel off the foil. Be *sure* that the bread is done; it is very easy to underbake this bread. Cool the loaves completely before wrapping them for the freezer. The bread will slice more easily if stored in the freezer and then sliced immediately after removing it. Otherwise, it has a tendency to crumble.

VARIATIONS:

More nuts make the bread better. Brown sugar can be substituted for part of the white. Candied orange peel can be added.

CRANBERRY CHUTNEY

Here is something you can serve with pride with almost any kind of game dish. It will keep well in the fridge, too.

Mix together thoroughly 2 cups finely chopped lowbush cranberries, 2 tablespoons finely chopped chives or onions, ½ cup seedless raisins, 1 cup brown sugar, 2 tablespoons lemon juice, and 1 teaspoon salt. Keep the chutney in the refrigerator overnight or longer in order for the flavors to be well blended. Any leftover chutney can be stored in the refrigerator for up to 1 month.

UNCOOKED CRANBERRY SAUCE

It seems incredible that lowbush cranberries will thicken and jell and keep almost indefinitely, but they will. Some people call this uncooked cranberry sauce "relish." By whatever name, it is the best thing to serve with poultry.

Sort and clean the lowbush cranberries carefully. Discard any that are still green or that are blatantly overripe. Rinse in cold water and allow to drain thoroughly. Measure the berries into a large bowl or kettle, along with the juice from 1 or 2 oranges. Add half as much sugar as you have cranberries and stir well. Let stand for several hours, stirring about once each hour. At the end of this time, ladle the mixture into jelly glasses or fruit jars, seal, and store in a cool place.

A variation is to grind the cleaned berries with a whole orange, skin and all, and then add the sugar.

WILD RASPBERRY CAKE

Who would have thought one could make a cake using wild raspberries? It seems we will try almost anything when it comes to cookery.

Prepare 1 package Betty Crocker White Cake mix according to the directions on the box. Bake in a shallow rectangular pan. Next, prepare 1 package raspberry gelatin as directed on the box and pour it into another pan that is the same size as the cake pan. Chill the gelatin. When it is set, unmold it onto the cake top. Spread the top and sides with 1 pint sweetened whipped cream. Sweeten 2 cups of raspberries to taste and sprinkle them over the whipped cream. Cut in squares to serve.

CLOUDBERRY WHIP

In some areas of the state cloudberries are plentiful enough to make use of them in desserts such as the one described below. These berries are the same ones that the Eskimos call salmonberries.

Whip 1 cup heavy cream until stiff and fold it into about 3 ounces of marshmallow whip. Blend gently but thoroughly, then fold in ¾ cup cloudberries that have been crushed and flavored with a dash of ground ginger. Add ¼ cup finely chopped nuts, saving a few to sprinkle on top of each serving. Pour the mixture into an ice cube tray and freeze. Serve in parfait glasses with either a sprinkle of nuts or a perfect berry on top. The velvety texture of this dessert is particularly good served between two waffles with fruit syrup on top.

Other berries can be used as substitutes for cloudberries. True salmonberries, raspberries, blueberries, and strawberries would all do as well.

JAM ROLLS

These little roll-ups are a welcome addition to any lunch box and they make good picnic fare, too. They are a bit on the rich side, though, so watch yourself!

Preheat the oven to 450°F. Make up a batch of your favorite pie crust mix according to the instructions on the package. Roll out the dough on a lightly floured board and cut into strips measuring about 3 by 5 inches. Spread with butter or margarine and then with any wild berry jam. Sprinkle chopped walnuts or pecans over the jam. Roll the rectangles up like miniature jelly rolls and bake for 18 to 25 minutes, or until a rich golden brown.

BERRY PANDOWDY

You may choose from blueberries, raspberries, or lowbush cranberries for this fine dessert. The cranberries will require nearly double the amount of sugar, though.

Combine 4 cups berries, 1 cup sugar, and 2 tablespoons lemon juice and pour into a 9-inch-square pan. Preheat the oven to 375°F. Prepare the cake batter (either yellow or white cake) according to package directions. Spread the batter over the berry mixture in the pan. Sprinkle ½ cup finely chopped almonds over the top. Bake for 20 to 25 minutes, or until browned nicely. Cut in squares and serve while still warm, topped with real cream.

BERRY MOUSSE

Any of the sweeter wild (or cultivated) berries will be great in this mousse. Our choice would be wild strawberries if you can find enough of them. Cloudberries, salmonberries, or blueberries all would be fine as well.

In a medium-size saucepan stir together ¾ cup milk, 1 cup coconut flakes, and 2 envelopes unflavored gelatin. Cook and stir over medium heat until the gelatin is completely dissolved. Remove from the heat and stir a small amount of the hot mixture into 4 egg yolks, beating well. Then stir the warmed yolks into the coconut mixture and return to the heat for 1 minute, stirring constantly. Add ¼ teaspoon almond extract. Pour into a large mixing bowl and chill until the mixture will mound on a spoon. Meanwhile, beat 4 egg whites with ¼ teaspoon cream of tartar until foamy. Gradually add ⅔ cup sugar, beating constantly until stiff peaks form.

Gently fold the egg whites, a purée of 1 pint of your choice of berries, and 1 cup whipping cream, whipped, into the yolk mixture. Spoon into your nicest serving dish and chill for several hours or overnight.

WILD BERRY SYRUPS

Wild currants, blueberries, and raspberries all make excellent syrups. These syrups are used by many Alaskans on hotcakes, French toast, waffles, ice cream, and as an ingredient in wonderful summer coolers. The currant syrup is especially good in lemonade.

There really isn't much to making these syrups. The hardest part is the harvesting. When you get the berries home, sort and clean them, but do not wash them unless it is really necessary. Some of their good juice would be washed away if you did. Mash the berries with a potato masher and put them in a large preserving kettle. Add barely enough water to keep them from scorching and cook slowly until the juice seems to be extracted. Add small amounts of water from time to time if it is really needed. Remove from the heat when the berries have given up their juice and set aside to cool. Drain the juice through a jelly bag or similar contraption. Be careful not to squeeze the bag, or the juice will be cloudy instead of clear. Allow to drain overnight.

Measure out the juice. Add one-half as much sugar as you have juice and place both in a large kettle. Bring to a boil and reduce the heat to simmer. Simmer slowly for about half an hour, stirring it occasionally to prevent scorching.

This syrup will keep for several

weeks in the refrigerator, but not indefinitely. If you have only small amounts of berries you can combine 2 or 3 kinds and make a delicious syrup. Lowbush cranberry, cloudberry, and salmonberry are all good bases for syrup.

WILD BERRY SHORTCAKE

In our opinion, there is no shortcake as good as that made with pie crust. Other kinds are not really "short" at all. Try making this recipe with Betty Crocker pie crust mix in the stick form. It's very easy to mix and bake.

Wild raspberries, salmonberries, or blueberries are all excellent in this shortcake, but cranberries are too sour. Try to gather your berries away from a road, where they will not be dusty; that way they won't lose their luscious juice in washing. Just crush them and add a few drops of juice from the homestead lemon (or lime). Use enough sugar to sweeten the berries, but not so much as to "drown" their delicious wild taste. Make a pie crust, following the directions on the package, and bake it. Put the berries on the crust while it is still slightly warm and the juice will soak in better.

If you are really lucky you might find enough wild strawberries to make a shortcake. Of course, there is no law against using cultivated strawberries, either.

ROSE HIPS (ROSE FRUIT)

The farther north you go, the more vitamin C the rose hips have. Rose hips are extremely valuable to people in the bush who don't have access to oranges, fresh or canned. They should be gathered in late summer before the frost strikes, though they can still be used even after they are frosted and soft.

To prepare rose hip juice for use in many things, just snap the stems and tails off the rose hips and cook in enough water to almost cover them. Cook until well softened. Put through a sieve. Cook again in less water and again put through a sieve. Repeat once more. Then discard any remaining seeds and skins and drain the rest overnight through a jelly bag or several layers of cheesecloth. The juice can be made into syrup or just stored in the refrigerator in a covered jar, to use from time to time in various concoctions that would benefit from the addition of vitamin C. The pulp can be used in jam or jelly to augment the quantity where you are a bit short and to add vitamin C.

Use rose hip juice in any syrup, jam, or jelly in place of water — at least partly. It doesn't have much taste, so it can be used in a lot of different things to add that all-important vitamin C.

One use for the pulp is to spread it thinly on cookie sheets and dry it in a slow oven, with the oven door slightly open to allow moisture to escape. When completely dry, break the sheet of purée into smaller pieces and pulverize with a rolling pin. The resulting powder is delicious sprinkled on cereal or in beverages, or used in place of a little flour in many recipes.

JUNIPER SAUCE

Hunters often bring home a pocketful of juniper berries along with their moose or caribou. They seem to ripen about hunt-

ing time, though it actually takes them 2 or 3 years to ripen and turn dark. Juniper does not have true berries — they are really a species of cone — but they resemble berries.

You are fortunate if you found and collected a quantity of juniper berries in the fall and dried them thoroughly. They are just what you need for this sauce, which is so good served with game birds. Crush a few dry juniper berries between 2 sheets of waxed paper with a rolling pin. Make at least a couple of teaspoons full. Then heat 2 tablespoons butter or margarine until light brown, but not scorched. Stir in 2 tablespoons flour and continue stirring over low heat for 2 or 3 minutes. Now add a cup of game stock or bouillon and simmer for 15 minutes longer, stirring now and then. Then add about ½ cup Madeira wine, salt and pepper to taste, and the crushed juniper berries and simmer for 10 more minutes. If the sauce is a bit too thick to suit you, just add a little more stock, a spoonful at a time.

CANDIED ROSE HIPS

Rose hips are the seed vessels of the rose. We like to use them in as many ways as we can, for they are known to be extremely rich in vitamin C. Try to gather yours in the wild, away from dusty highways, just before the first frost is due to hit. These tidbits take quite a bit of work, but the result is well worth it.

Snap off the stems and tails of the wild rose hips you have collected. Discard any imperfect ones. Insects like rose hips, too, so sort them with care. Split the hips open. With a teaspoon turned over, force the seeds out of the hips. Scrape out any extrane-

ous membrane from the inside. Cover with cold water in a saucepan and bring to the boiling point. Reduce the heat and simmer slowly for 10 minutes. Drain well.

Cook to the boiling point 1 cup of sugar, ½ cup water, and 1 or 2 pieces of crystallized ginger. Add the drained rose hip pieces (not more than a cupful at a time). Cook slowly until the hips just begin to appear translucent. Using a skimmer, remove the hips from the syrup and spread them on a platter to cool. If you have more hips, cook them in the same way until all are cooked, but never add more than a cupful at a time. When cool, roll the hips in granulated sugar and spread thinly on waxed paper to dry. These make a healthful snack for the kids. They should be stored in an airtight, kidproof glass container.

HIGHBUSH CRANBERRY CATSUP

This stuff can be used almost anywhere that commercial catsup is used, and it is much better with game than the commercial brands. We have enough highbush cranberries in Alaska so that everyone could make it. It is especially good with shish kebabs or in marinades for game. It is even excellent with fish and other seafood. Versatile, indeed.

Cook together until soft 1 pound chopped onions, 4 pounds highbush cranberries, and 2 cups water. Rub through a sieve, then add the following: 2 cups vinegar; 2 cups white sugar; 2 cups dark brown sugar; 1 tablespoon each ground cloves, cinnamon, allspice, and salt; and 1 teaspoon pepper. Boil until thick, pour into hot sterilized jars, and seal.

JUST WEEDS:
Edible Wild Plants and Mushrooms

Such plants as nettle, dandelion, sourgrass, fireweed, and many others are often spoken of as "just weeds." Yet these and many other species of plants in the north are edible; not only will eating them save us money, but they are exceedingly healthful. We are including wild mushrooms in this chapter, even though they are really fungi. There is nothing better than properly prepared wild mushrooms, but you must be sure of your species since there are some deadly ones in the north. And some are lookalikes.

FREEZING MUSHROOMS

If you run across large patches of edible mushrooms, as is sometimes the case, gather and freeze what you don't eat right away. Puffballs and shaggy manes are particularly good when frozen for later use.

Clean and trim the mushrooms and slice them in 2 or more pieces of fairly uniform size. Bring a large kettle of water to a rolling boil. Put about a cupful of mushrooms at a time in a colander and immerse in the boiling water for about 30 seconds. Remove from the water and plunge the mushrooms into cold water to cool rapidly. Continue this process until all the mushrooms have been blanched. When all are completely cooled, they may be thoroughly drained, put in plastic bags, and stored in the freezer.

Another way to prepare mushrooms for the freezer is to sauté the pieces in butter or margarine instead of blanching. After sautéing, which should be brief, cool the pieces completely and enclose in plastic bags for freezer storage.

MUSHROOM AND POTATO PIE

This really isn't a pie, but what else would you call it? Whatever name it goes by, it is a good dish to serve with any meat.

Boil white potatoes and yams (4 parts potatoes to 1 part yams) together until soft. Mash and season as for regular mashed potatoes. Sauté freshly gathered puffballs that are crisp and

white inside, sliced into 2 or more pieces. Add as many of these as you like to the mashed potatoes. Place in a fairly deep casserole. Melt a couple of tablespoons butter or margarine and add to it ½ cup fine dry bread crumbs. Mix well. Sprinkle the ingredients of the casserole with minced wild chives, parsley, or chervil. Then scatter the crumbs over the top. Bake in a preheated 350°F. oven for about 30 minutes, or until nicely browned and crusty.

ALASKA SALAD

The assortment of "weeds" called for in the recipe below may not all be available to you at one time, but procure what you can. They are not all absolutely essential.

Wash the greens listed below in cold water. Dry them on paper towels and tear them into small pieces — enough for the number of people you plan to serve and with as much variety as possible. Endive, young dandelion, Swiss chard, collards, fireweed, chicory, and sorrel can all be arranged in a suitable salad bowl. Mix 1 cup sour cream with about 1 tablespoon tomato purée in a smaller bowl; beat until creamy, then pour over the greens in the larger bowl. Toss the salad until the greens are well coated with the dressing. Garnish with tomatoes plucked from your greenhouse and cut in wedges. Sprinkle snipped wild chives over the top.

The dressing for this summery salad can be varied by beating 1 tablespoon of honey into it along with the purée.

MUSHROOM SALAD

This easy and delicious mushroom salad can be made 2 or 3 hours before serving and kept in the refrigerator, thus saving you time when you need it most.

Put 1 cup French dressing in a bowl. Clean and slice 2½ cups fresh firm puffballs. Slice them thinly and drop into the dressing immediately. This will prevent the discoloration that often takes place when puffballs are cut. Season with salt and pepper and any fresh or dried herbs you prefer. Wild chives, green onions, parsley, chervil, and thyme are all good with puffballs — either singly or in combination. A few minutes before serving time, remove the seasoned mushrooms from the refrigerator, drain, and serve on nests of salad greens with toast triangles.

PUFFBALL SALAD

There are times when one finds enough little puffball mushrooms to make many dishes and even to dry and freeze some of them. But this elegant salad is one of the most appreciated recipes.

This is essentially a green salad, and any good salad greens will do. Use spinach, lettuce, and various wild greens singly or in combination. Chickweed from your garden, fireweed shoots, dandelion leaves (young, of course), watercress, chives, and spring beauty are all good. Be sure to wash any greens well and spin

them dry if possible. Greens should be torn into small pieces. Sprinkle a small amount of sugar and scatter a few salad croutons over the greens.

Clean the puffballs and slice as necessary. They must be sliced at least once to be sure you are not getting a baby amanita, which is deadly. The puffball will be pure white inside and have no sign of the embryo of another mushroom. Use oil and lemon juice for the dressing — quite scantily — and toss the puffballs and greens lightly.

HAM WITH PUFFBALLS

Always remember that even small puffballs must be sliced in two to be certain there is no sign of the deadly amanita embryo lurking inside. Puffballs are pure white inside and resemble a crisp marshmallow.

Cook puffballs or other edible mushrooms in salted water after they have been thoroughly cleaned and sliced into roughly equal-size pieces. Add a squirt from the homestead lemon. Cook over medium heat for a few minutes until tender. Remove from the heat and drain well. Cut cooked ham into ½-inch cubes. Stir the mushrooms and ham into a previously prepared White Sauce (p.91). Add several pieces of wild chives, snipped quite small, and black pepper. Any other seasoning you may wish can be used — just remember that mushrooms have a delicate flavor of their own, which should not be overpowered with seasonings. Serve over hot baking-powder biscuits.

To vary, you can use gameburger or cubed and cooked game meat, but the ham seems to be ideal with this.

PUFFBALL SAUTÉ

When a warm day comes along after some rainy ones in late summer it is time to keep watch out for puffballs. They go well with almost anything, but they are at their best just sautéed and served by themselves.

Wipe the puffballs with a damp paper towel, but do not wash them unless really necessary. Be sure that each one is sliced in two at least once to make certain that it does not have an embryo of the deadly amanita within. A real puffball is pure white inside with absolutely no markings of any kind. The size of the skillet and the amount of butter or margarine you melt in it depends entirely upon the quantity of puffballs you are cooking. (About 2 tablespoons margarine for 1 cup of sliced puffballs will be sufficient to start with. More can be added as they cook if needed.) The mushroom pieces should not be crowded in the heavy skillet. Instead of stirring the puffballs as they cook, try shifting the skillet back and forth rapidly to keep the pieces moving.

Season as you wish. We like just a little chicken soup base added to the margarine, a hint of black pepper, a smidgen of salt, and marjoram. Sometimes we vary it with other herbs or a little sherry. But remember: puffballs have a delicate natural flavor that must not be overwhelmed with seasoning. Cook over medium heat for just 2 or 3 minutes. Green peas in White Sauce (p. 91) go well with these.

MUSHROOM SOUP

When harvesting wild mushrooms avoid gathering too many at one time. They do

not keep well even in the refrigerator, so they should be used or processed for the freezer the same day they are picked. Don't collect any that appear to be over-ripe and be careful not to get any of the inedible ones. It is best to go mushroom hunting with someone who is knowledgeable about fungi if you are not familiar with them yourself.

Clean and trim the mushrooms (puffballs preferred) as needed and sauté quickly in butter or margarine. You will need to slice them into fairly small pieces and even the smallest must be cut in two at least once. Make a rich White Sauce (p. 91), using half-and-half instead of milk and seasoning it with a little chicken soup base. Add other seasonings to taste, then gently stir in the mushroom pieces. Simmer over low heat for 10 minutes. Serve with toast points or croutons.

Instead of sautéing the mushroom pieces, you can also put them in a saucepan with a little water — just enough to cover — and a lump of margarine. Bring to a boil and reduce the heat to simmer. Cook until most of the water has been cooked away. Now make the White Sauce as above. While it is cooking, put the mushrooms through a sieve. When the sauce is ready stir in the sieved mushrooms. This makes a delicious creamy soup.

PAN-FRIED MORELS

Morel mushrooms are mighty fine prepared in this fashion, but be sure they are the true morels. They have cousins that are inedible. If it is too late for morels, you can use puffballs or other of the edible mushrooms that pop up in late August and September.

Melt margarine over medium-high heat in a large frying pan. Clean, trim, and slice as many mushrooms as necessary and add them to the pan. Season with white pepper, 1 clove garlic (crushed or minced), and salt. A few grains of nutmeg will also go well, especially with the morels. Fry briefly, stirring with the back of a pancake turner; then add a little cooking sherry. Stir once more; sprinkle with paprika or finely chopped parsley. Serve with small toast points.

FRENCH-FRIED SHAGGY MANE MUSHROOMS

Inky caps can be used in this recipe, too. Either one will be super served with a good moose or caribou steak. Strangely enough, these mushrooms seem to mature during hunting season. Be sure they are in their prime before using them — too old and they will be no good. Young solid ones are what you will need to pick. Use them the same day they are gathered, since they do not keep, even in the refrigerator.

To mix the batter, beat 2 eggs well with a rotary egg beater, then beat into them ¾ cup milk. Sift together and add 1 cup flour, 1 teaspoon baking powder, and ½ teaspoon salt. Stir to blend, then beat well. Add 1 teaspoon melted shortening. The batter should be thick enough to coat onion rings and mushrooms evenly and thoroughly.

Select small, solid fresh mushrooms (shaggy manes or inky caps). Trim and clean as needed. Dip in the batter and fry quickly in deep fat heated to 375°F. Serve with French-fried onion rings. Prepare the onion rings first and keep them hot in the oven, spread out on a baking sheet.

NEW POTATOES WITH CHIVES

Do you have wild chives growing in your garden? They transplant easily and will grow in almost any kind of soil. And they are so good to have on hand. When the season for using them fresh is over, you will no doubt find some in your freezer or some that have been freeze-dried from your own garden.

Scrape off the skins of enough freshly dug new potatoes to feed your crowd. Put on to boil and cook rather slowly, until the potatoes test done when pierced with the point of a sharp knife. While the new potatoes are cooking, cut several leaves from your chive plants and snip them into small bits with kitchen scissors. Melt enough margarine or butter to pour over the potatoes. Add a few squirts from the homestead lemon or lime and mix with the chives. Then drench the potatoes in this sauce.

CREAM OF CHIVES SOUP

Cut the tubular leaves of wild chives in the spring, when they have not been up long enough to be too tough or too strong. Also snip a few fireweed tops that are still that dark maroon color. They both spring up about the same time around here.

Snip the chives into small bits — about ¼ cupful per person — and a few sprigs of the fireweed, too, if available. Cook together in a little water over low heat until the chive pieces are soft. As they cook, add about a level teaspoon of chicken soup base per person, a little margarine or butter, a very little sea salt, some pepper, a dash of cayenne, marjoram, thyme, and any other seasonings you wish.

When the chives are tender add milk or half-and-half — about ½ cup per person or less. Bring to a boil and stir in some Betty Crocker Potato Buds — about 2 tablespoons per person. Remove from the heat and allow to set for a minute. Pour into soup bowls and serve with croutons or Herbed French Bread (p.87).

A GOOD VARIATION: If the hunter in the family brings in but one spruce grouse, cook it until tender in a small amount of water. Remove the meat from the bones and shred. Use the liquid to cook the chives in and proceed as before. Add the shredded grouse meat to the soup when you add the milk.

CHIVE TURNOVERS

Here is something a bit different to have with your eggs and bacon on a sunny Sunday morning.

Mix up a batch of your favorite biscuits, following the directions on the package. Roll out to the approximate size and thickness of pancakes.

Chop and sauté in margarine a cupful, or thereabouts, of wild chives — the young and tender foliage. Stir-fry them for a couple of minutes. Season with sea salt, black pepper, and a little (*very* little) dried jalapeño pepper. Put a spoonful of the chive mixture on one half of each doughy round. Fold so that it is a turnover. Seal the edges tightly by moistening them with milk and pressing together with a floured fork. Bake on a cookie sheet in a preheated 450°F. oven for 10 to 12 minutes. These may be prepared ahead of time, in quantity and reheated in aluminum foil just before serving. You can also make them in miniature to serve as hors d'oeuvres.

EGG IN A NEST

If you are tired of eating eggs the same old way you might want to try this recipe. Springtime is the season when the wild plants are at their best — young and tender.

Butter individual baking dishes. In each dish put 2 tablespoons of cooked wild greens. Use one kind only. Suitable ones would be dandelion leaves, fireweed shoots, and nettle tops. Chop them finely before putting into the baking dishes and season them to taste. Sprinkle the greens liberally with grated Parmesan cheese. Break an egg into each little casserole and pour on 1 tablespoon heavy cream. Sprinkle with more grated cheese. Bake in a preheated 350°F. oven for 7 to 10 minutes, or until the eggs are set. Watch them closely for the last 3 or 4 minutes of cooking.

FIDDLEHEADS

Every spring we used to go up along the Parks Highway between Anchorage and Fairbanks to collect fiddleheads to freeze. Acres of them were available then, and there must be a lot of them still. But they have to be gathered at just the right time. We have seen frozen ones in the markets and occasionally fresh ones, too.

If your fiddleheads are fresh, you'll need to peel off the woolly, rusty-looking skin from around the bottom. If they are frozen, thaw them partially before cooking. Wash the fiddleheads (called fiddlenecks by some people) well and drain thoroughly. Cook as you would fresh asparagus, for about 5 to 8 minutes. Don't overcook. Fiddleheads can be a gourmet dish, but they need to be handled simply. Most people prefer them merely salted, but you may like additional seasoning; don't use too much, though. Pour a little melted butter over the cooked fiddleheads. Sometimes melted cheese can be used instead if used sparingly.

SPRING SALAD

Mother nature provides us with a whole variety of plants that are useful for making salads. Here are a few of them: chives (both foliage and roots), wild celery, wild spinach, spring beauty, scurvygrass, fireweed, sourgrass, sourdock, roseroot or king's crown, and the ever-present dandelion. Learn to identify them, and also learn which ones you like together. There are others, too, including rose petals and violet flowers and leaves.

Choose several of your favorite wild plants that are in the young and tender stage to use for your spring salad. We always use chives, some fireweed shoots just coming through the ground, and a few others. Don't be afraid to make use of a little lettuce if you like. An oil-and-vinegar dressing is best on this type of green salad. By using different combinations of greens you can vary the salad each time you make it. Try adding a few dandelion "buttons." The buttons are the tight, unopened blossoms.

FIREWEED SALAD

Early in the season the fireweed stems break easier than later on, so I just snap them off. Later I use a knife and clip them against my thumb. Use only the tops, for they will be tender even on a mature plant.

I generally collect a batch of fireweed and dip it in the lake in front of my

cabin. You might call it washing, but the real reason is to get a little water on them to dilute the vinegar.

I bunch the fireweed in one hand and use a sharp knife to cross-cut it into short lengths (easier and faster than chopping in a bowl). Then I score an onion and dice it finely onto the cut fireweed. Chopped dry onion works about as well. Add some finely diced raw potato, some carrots, pickle, or whatever. Then, using a fork and a sharp knife, I chop the bowl contents again. Next add some sugar (be generous), salt, black pepper, a little chili powder, and some garlic powder or garlic salt. Add enough vinegar so that you have some juice in the bowl at the last serving. Mix up the salad and taste it for seasoning. Make any necessary adjustments at this point.

Now I add some Cheddar cheese diced finely and a bit of chopped lunchmeat and mix again. Sprinkle on a dash of paprika for color. Often as not I sprinkle on some brown sugar after everything else is in.

– *Dick Proenneke*

GOOSETONGUE GREENS

Goosetongue is sometimes called wild spinach, particularly in southeastern Alaska. If you can find a patch where it isn't too dusty, you are in for a treat.

Gather the goosetongue and wash it carefully in a couple of changes of water, lifting out of the water slowly to rinse out sand or debris. Cook it just as you would spinach from your own garden. It will need almost no water to cook in — just the water that clings to it after washing should be sufficient. Serve with your choice of seasonings and a couple of hard-cooked eggs, sliced over the top. A pleasing variation is to serve it cold with the eggs and mayonnaise. Try it both ways.

WILTED WILD GREENS

Alaska's wild vegetables grow in great variety, but rarely does one kind grow in one place in great abundance. Isn't it fortunate that they mix together so well?

Gather young and tender wild greens such as fireweed, nettles, sorrel, dandelion, and others. Wash them thoroughly through at least 2 changes of lukewarm water — lifting them carefully from the last water in order to let any sand or soil settle to the bottom of the container. Allow the greens to dry a little on several thicknesses of paper towels. While they are drying, fry several strips of bacon until crisp; lift out of the frying pan and crumble. To the bacon drippings in the pan, add 2 tablespoons vinegar, 2 tablespoons water, a dash of salt and pepper, and 1 tablespoon brown sugar. Also add any other seasonings that you think might be good with this. Bring the mixture quickly to a boil and add the crumbled bacon. Place the greens in a salad bowl and pour the bacon mixture over them. Toss just a little to mingle the ingredients. Finely chopped hard-cooked eggs may be added if desired.

SASSY SOURDOUGH:
Sourdough from Start to Finish

Whoever first discovered sourdough did us all a great service. It is too bad that more people don't take advantage of sourdough cookery and use it for their daily bread. Besides bread, it starts rolls, hotcakes, cookies, cake, and other goodies. It is a bit more trouble than baking the regular bread products or than going to the supermarket, but try keeping a sourdough pot going. You won't be sorry.

BASIC SOURDOUGH STARTER

There are several ways to start a starter, but this is as good as any and not a difficult one. Just remember not to mix or store your sourdough starter in metal containers.

Stir well 2 cups white flour, 2 scant cups of water that is barely warm, and 1 package dry yeast or a yeast cake, crumbled. Set in a warm place (not too warm) or a closed cupboard overnight and allow to work. This is called the sponge.

In the morning put ½ cup of the starter in a scalded pint jar with a tight cover and store in a cool place. This is your Sourdough Starter. The remaining batter can be used immediately for hotcakes, waffles, bread, cake, or in other sourdough recipes.

WARNING: Be sure always to save at least ½ cup of the starter for future use and always to store it in a cool place. Do this before starting any other sourdough recipe.

SOURDOUGH BREAD

This is the basic sourdough white bread and variations of it are legion. After you have gotten the knack of making good white bread, feel free to experiment.

Set a sponge as for hotcakes and let stand overnight, or at least 8 hours, in a warm place. After the usual saving out of ½ cup of starter, sift 4 cups flour, 1 teaspoon salt, and 2 teaspoons sugar into a large mixing bowl. Make a well in the center. Add 2 tablespoons melted shortening to the sponge and put it into the well of the flour mixture. Mix gradually, adding more flour if needed to make a soft dough. Turn out on a lightly floured board and knead for 10 to 15 minutes.

Do not skimp on the kneading. Place in a large greased bowl, turning to get all surfaces in contact with the grease. Cover with a clean kitchen towel and set in a warm place until double in bulk.

Punch the dough down and shape into 1 large or 2 smaller loaves. After putting the dough in the bread pans, again cover and set in a warm place to rise once more. Bake in a preheated 375°F. oven for 10 minutes; reduce the heat to 350°F. and continue baking until done, which should be in about an hour. The loaves should give off a hollow sound when thumped if they are done. When the loaves test right, turn them out on racks to cool and brush them all over with melted shortening or salad oil.

SOURDOUGH KNOTS OR STICKS

Breadsticks, pretzel shapes, and simple knots are fun to make and bake. They go well with soups and stews and other such recipes. Vary the recipe by rolling the unbaked sticks in sesame seeds or finely chopped nuts or by adding chervil flakes or dried minced onions and kneading them in.

Use any good basic sourdough bread recipe. After the first rising of the dough, pinch off large pieces and roll them out to a ½-inch thickness on a slightly floured board. These pieces can then be cut into ½-inch widths in any length you like. Make plain breadsticks or knots or other shapes if you wish. Roll the strips a little in your fingers to round them and place them on lightly greased cookie sheets about an inch apart. Let them rest for half an hour, then brush lightly with luke-warm water and bake in a preheated 400°F. oven for about 18 to 20 minutes, or until well browned.

BUTTERMILK SOURDOUGH BREAD

This recipe makes 4 loaves — you can divide the quantities in half if you like. We don't like to go to the effort of baking bread for just a few loaves.

Take your sourdough starter out of the refrigerator and set your sponge the night before you plan to bake the bread. To set the sponge, add 1 cup flour and 1 cup lukewarm water to the starter. Set aside the sponge to work in a warm, draft-free place for 8 hours, or overnight.

Measure 12 cups flour into a large bowl. I generally use 8 cups unbleached white flour, 2 cups whole wheat flour, and 2 cups oat flour. I have used other combinations, depending on what kinds I had on hand, but I always use more of the white flour than of the other kinds so the bread isn't too heavy.

In another container combine 3 cups buttermilk, 8 tablespoons butter or margarine, 8 tablespoons honey, and 1½ teaspoons salt. Heat the mixture to lukewarm. While the buttermilk mixture is heating, dissolve 1 package active dry yeast in ¼ cup warm water.

Add 1 cup of the sourdough sponge to the warm buttermilk mixture. Return the rest of the sourdough starter to the refrigerator to be ready for the next baking. Add the buttermilk mixture and dissolved yeast to the flour. Mix thoroughly to make a fairly stiff dough. Knead until smooth and elastic. Place in a greased bowl

and turn the ball of dough so that all parts come in contact with the grease. Let rise for about 1 hour, or until double in bulk. Punch the dough down, divide it into 4 parts, place in greased loaf pans, and let rise again for about 45 minutes. Bake at 350°F. for 30 to 35 minutes, or until the loaves sound hollow when you tap them. This bread is especially good toasted. – *A. Friend*

SOURDOUGH PAN ROLLS

We like to have several plastic bags full of these rolls in the freezer. They come in handy on all sorts of occasions. These are the rolls we use in our recipe for Broiled Gameburger Rolls (p. 51).

Use the recipe for Sourdough Bread (p. 82) or Sourdough French Bread (p. 85) to make these. Instead of putting the loaves in the pans after the first rising, form long, loaflike rolls and cut them into 2½- to 3-inch pieces. Place them side by side (but an inch apart) in well-greased shallow pans. Cover with a clean kitchen towel and let them rise in a warm place until double in bulk. Bake in a preheated 400°F. oven for 10 minutes to set the crust; then reduce the heat to 350°F. and bake for 35 to 40 minutes longer. Check on them frequently near the end of the baking period.

A good variation is to pinch off much smaller pieces of the dough and place them 3 to each well-greased muffin cup. Let rise and bake as above. These form clover-leaf rolls.

BURGER BUNS

When we prepare our meat for the freezer we always make a lot of burger because it can be used in so many ways. It has proved to be a real lifesaver many times. For making burger sandwiches we need buns, of course, and these sourdough buns, baked complete with onions, are great.

Bring ½ cup water to a boil and mix with ¼ cup milk. Cool to lukewarm. Sift and measure 2½ cups flour with 1 teaspoon salt and 1 tablespoon sugar into a large bowl. Melt 1 tablespoon shortening. Make a well in the middle of the dry ingredients and pour into it the liquids, including the melted shortening, and 1 cup sourdough starter. Mix thoroughly. Cover with a clean kitchen towel, set in a slightly warm place, and let rise until double in bulk.

Turn out the dough onto a lightly floured surface and knead vigorously for 3 or 4 minutes; then roll out the dough to a ½-inch thickness. Cut into 3-inch circles. (You can improvise a 3-inch cutter, out of a tin can or other object, that will be about regulation bun size.) Spread softened margarine or butter on half of the circles. Sprinkle them with minced dried onion and put an unbuttered circle on top. Place on a greased cookie sheet, cover, and let rise again until double in bulk. Place in a 375°F. oven for 10 minutes. Reduce the heat to 350°F. and continue baking until the buns are done (about 30 minutes).

When you cook your moose-burgers, all you have to do is lift the top off of a bun and there it is already buttered and with the onions right there, too. These buns can be frozen, of course, as can other sourdough items.

SOURDOUGH FRENCH BREAD

This is our favorite of all the sourdough products and it is not too difficult to make, either. A little practice and you'll bake perfect bread every time.

Set your sponge the night before you plan to bake the French bread. Add 1½ cups each flour and water to the starter you reserved after your last baking. Set in a warm place to work overnight. When you are ready to proceed with the bread baking the next day, bring to a boil 1 cup water; when it has cooled to lukewarm, add to it ½ cup milk and 2 tablespoons melted margarine; mix well. Stir in 1½ cups of the sponge you set the night before and return the rest to the refrigerator. In a large mixing bowl, sift 5 cups white flour with 2 teaspoons salt and 2 tablespoons sugar. Make a well in the center and stir the sponge mixture into it, gradually dampening all the flour. Cover with a clean kitchen towel and set in a warm place to rise until double in bulk. Turn the dough out onto a lightly floured board but do not knead the French bread. Instead, divide the dough into two equal portions. Roll each half into a ¾-inch-thick rectangle. Fold the two long sides of one rectangle toward the middle and then roll up as you would a jelly roll. Repeat with the second rectangle. Sprinkle a well-greased cookie sheet with coarse cornmeal and place the two loaves on the sheet. With kitchen shears make several diagonal slashes on top of each. Again cover with a towel and let rise until double in bulk. Bake in a preheated 350°F. oven for 10 minutes. Reduce the heat to 325°F. and continue baking for 45 minutes, or until done. Remove from the oven and brush the tops liberally with shortening. Transfer to racks to cool.

PARKER HOUSE SOURDOUGH ROLLS

For some reason, we don't see those good Parker House rolls in bakeries much anymore. Maybe this recipe will help make up for that lack.

Using the Sourdough French Bread recipe above, proceed as before to the rolling-out stage. Then roll the dough to a ½-inch thickness and cut out with a round cookie cutter. Make a crease across the center of each round with the back of a knife blade. Brush the rounds with melted butter or margarine and fold over on the crease. Place the rolls close together on a well-greased cookie sheet. Cover with a clean kitchen towel and let rise until nearly double in bulk. Bake in a preheated 350°F. oven for 5 minutes, then reduce the heat to 325°F. and continue baking until done. Remove from the oven and brush generously with melted butter or margarine; transfer to a rack to cool.

SOURDOUGH BRAIDS

Braids make a nice breakfast bread and are easy enough to prepare. You can vary

this recipe by shaping the dough into butterhorns instead of braids.

Follow the Sourdough French Bread recipe above for these and proceed as before until you reach the rolling-out stage. Then roll the dough to a ½-inch thickness. Brush with melted butter or margarine and then cut into strips about ¾ inch wide and 12 to 14 inches long. Seal 3 of these strips at one end by pinching them together tightly, and then proceed to braid them and seal the finished ends. Work directly on a greased cookie sheet, as it is difficult to move the braids and still have them retain their shape. Cover the braids and let them rise until double in bulk. Bake in a preheated 350°F. oven for 5 minutes, then reduce the heat to 325°F. and continue baking for about 20 minutes.

While the braids are baking, prepare a glaze of ½ cup powdered sugar mixed with 1½ teaspoons water. Also have ready ½ cup chopped nuts. When the braids are done, remove from the oven and brush their tops with melted shortening. Transfer to a cooling rack and drizzle glaze over them. At this point you will have to work rapidly, or the glaze will set before the nuts are sprinkled on.

SOURDOUGH HOTCAKES

Hotcakes are about the most popular of all sourdough recipes, and rightly so. If you have any left over they make good sandwiches to take on the trail, and some birds really go for them in a big way when they are broken into pieces.

Hotcake starter must be set aside the night before it is to be used. Place the starter in a crockery mixing bowl and add 2 cups warm water and 2 cups flour. Beat vigorously and set in a warm (not hot) place to ripen overnight. In the morning it will have nearly doubled in bulk, will be bubbly, and have that characteristic yeasty scent. Now is the time to save out that ½ cup of starter for the next time. To the remaining sponge add 1 or 2 eggs, 2 teaspoons baking soda, 1 teaspoon salt, and 1 tablespoon sugar.

Fry on a hot griddle, turning once, just as you would any hotcake batter. Serve with a good topping such as melted wildberry jelly, jam, or maple syrup.

Vary your recipe occasionally by adding ½ cup whole wheat or buckwheat flour, cornmeal, bran flakes, or the like. The second egg mentioned above will provide the additional liquid needed to absorb this extra half cup of dry ingredient.

SOURDOUGH WAFFLES

How about crisp bacon, eggs, sourdough waffles, and wild blueberry syrup for a good breakfast? We don't think it could be much better; the blueberry flavor will remind you of summertime, when you plucked the berries. Here's how to make the waffles.

Set the sponge as you did for hotcakes except use ½ cup more flour. Let the sponge stand overnight. Remove the usual ½ cup of starter for the next time around. To the remaining sponge add 1 teaspoon each of salt and baking soda, 2 tablespoons sugar, and 2 eggs that have been beaten slightly. Mix well and add 4 tablespoons melted shortening. Grill in a waffle iron. Of course, these waffles are excellent for breakfast, but try them sometime for a Sunday supper served as a base

for creamed ham and mushrooms or creamed chicken.

CINNAMON ROLLS

By doubling this recipe you can make the mammoth cinnamon rolls that are so popular in bakeries these days. They are hard to manage when rolling up, though, so we stick to the smaller version.

Set the sourdough sponge 6 to 8 hours before using (overnight will do fine). Add 2 cups water and 2 cups flour to the starter. When the ripening process is complete sift 3¼ cups flour with ⅓ cup sugar and 1 teaspoon salt. Make a well in the center. In another bowl beat 2 eggs slightly, add 2 cups of the sponge, ¼ cup melted margarine, and ½ cup milk that has been scalded and then cooled. Pour into the well of the dry ingredients and mix lightly. Turn the dough out onto a floured board and knead until smooth and elastic, using only enough flour to make handling easy. Grease the bowl and return the dough to it, turning the dough as you do so in order to coat all surfaces with the grease. Cover with a clean kitchen towel and set in a warm place to double in bulk (about 1 to 2 hours).

Punch down the dough and again turn it out onto a lightly floured board. Roll into a large ½-inch-thick rectangle. Brush with ½ cup melted margarine. Sprinkle 3 tablespoons sugar, 1 tablespoon cinnamon, and ½ teaspoon ginger over the dough. Roll up quickly as you would a jelly roll and cut the roll into ¾-inch slices. Place the slices, cut-side down, in a well-greased baking pan. Set aside to rise until double in bulk. Bake in a preheated 350°F. oven for 20 to 25 minutes, or until well done. Turn out onto racks to cool. Drizzle with a glaze made of ½ cup confectioners' sugar, 2 teaspoons water, and a couple drops of lemon juice.

PECAN ROLLS

We like these even better than Cinnamon Rolls, and they are just as easy to make. Make plenty of them because they tend to disappear in a hurry.

Prepare the dough for Cinnamon Rolls (see recipe above). You may want to experiment with these and make them slightly smaller than the Cinnamon Rolls. We usually roll the punched-down dough into 2 rectangles and then proceed as before. The resulting rolls won't be as bulky. Sometimes we cut them only into ½-inch slices.

Pour ½ to 1 teaspoon melted butter or margarine into each cup of a muffin tin, then sprinkle in ½ teaspoon brown sugar and a few coarsely chopped pecans. Place a slice of the rolled-up dough in each muffin cup, set aside to rise, and bake in a preheated 350°F. oven for 15 to 20 minutes, depending on how thick you cut the slices. No glaze is necessary for these rolls. Cool upside down on a rack.

HERBED FRENCH BREAD

The French bread in this recipe should be Sourdough French Bread (p. 85) if possible. If not, be sure it is perfectly fresh bakery-made bread.

Soften 1 stick of margarine (or less) and add to it herbs of your choice. Snipped fresh or dried wild chives, chervil or parsley, and dried thyme leaves make a good combination. Pa-

prika used sparingly is good for its color. Onion or garlic powder may be used instead of chives, and so may chopped fresh green onions. Try marjoram instead of thyme occasionally.

Slice a loaf of French bread thickly and spread with your herb mixture. Put the slices back together in loaf form and wrap in aluminum foil. Place in a hot oven and heat for 10 to 15 minutes, or until the bread is heated through. This bread goes particularly well with seafood.

CHOCOLATE CAKE

Sourdough chocolate cake is hard to beat. It will stay moist and is a super-good keeper if it has a chance. But you had better hide it from the family if you want it to keep for very long!

Blend 1 cup thick sourdough starter with 1 cup water, 1½ cups flour, and ¼ cup nonfat dry milk; allow to ferment until it is bubbly and the clean sour-milk aroma can be detected. In a large mixing bowl cream ½ cup soft shortening and gradually stir in 1 cup brown sugar, 2 teaspoons cinnamon, ½ teaspoon salt, 1½ teaspoons baking soda, and 1 teaspoon vanilla. Add 2 eggs and beat well. Melt 3 squares of baking chocolate over hot water. Add the starter mix and the chocolate to the creamed ingredients. Mix on low speed in an electric mixer or beat 100 strokes by hand to blend. Grease and flour 2 layer-cake pans or 1 large loaf-cake pan. Pour the cake batter into the pans and bake in a preheated 350°F. oven until done (about 30 to 40 minutes). The cake should spring back when touched with a fingertip. Frost with your favorite icing.

For a differently textured cake and one with more bulk, try separating the eggs and adding only the yolks to the creamed mixture. Beat the whites until they form stiff peaks and fold them in gently last of all. Very good either way.

SOURDOUGH HERMITS

These cookies are moist and keep well, but you must count on the cookie jar being raided frequently. The hermits may also be stored in the freezer.

Combine 1 cup thick sourdough starter (return the rest of the starter to the refrigerator for later use), ¼ cup nonfat dry milk, 1 cup water, and 1½ cups flour. Stir to mingle. Cover with a clean kitchen towel and set aside to ripen for 2 or 3 hours, or until bubbly. When the sponge is ripe, cream ¾ cup margarine in a large bowl and gradually add ¾ cup sugar. Beat 2 eggs slightly and add to the sugar mixture, together with ½ cup molasses. Sift 1 cup whole wheat flour with 1 teaspoon cinnamon, ½ teaspoon allspice, and ¼ teaspoon cream of tartar and add as well.

Boil ¾ cup raisins in 1 cup water for 2 or 3 minutes; then drain and cool completely. Add the raisins and ½ cup chopped nuts to the flour-egg mixture and blend well. Add the starter mix and stir again gently — just enough to mix thoroughly. Do not beat. The resulting cookie dough should be slightly thicker than cake dough, but not as thick as drop-cookie dough. If needed, add more liquid or more flour to gain the correct consistency. Drop by teaspoonfuls onto well-greased cookie sheets. Allow plenty of space between the cookies, as they are supposed to spread and should be rather large and flat. Bake at 375°F. until well browned.

TAIL ENDS:
Items That Don't Fit Anywhere Else

These recipes have spilled over from the major part of the book but must be accommodated somewhere. Rhubarb, of course, is not a wild fruit, but it is so common here that it ought to be included in any book of Alaskan recipes. Marinades and sauces, too, are included to enhance dishes described in earlier chapters. And a few of our great vegetables deserve a little attention.

RHUBARB CRUMBLE

Rhubarb is one plant that seems to grow everywhere in Alaska. While it is not a wild plant, it is distinctly Alaskan because it is so common. It can even be seen growing in the yards of abandoned places where the cabin has long since burned down.

Cut the rhubarb into small pieces until you have about 4 cups. Spread this evenly in the bottom of a 7x11-inch baking pan. Sprinkle 1 cup sugar (or the equivalent in honey) and ½ package strawberry Jello (dry) over the top, then 1 package dry cake mix. (I use Jiffy white cake mix.) Pour over all 1 cup boiling water and drizzle 2 or 3 tablespoons melted margarine or butter over the contents of the pan. Bake for 1 hour in a 350°F. oven. Top with whipped cream or ice cream before serving.   – Lois Armstrong

RHUBARB CONSERVE

We like to use strawberry Jello here, but orange and lemon are good, too.

Mix together 4 cups finely diced rhubarb, 4 cups sugar, and 1 can (16 ounces) grated pineapple. Let stand overnight. Next morning, boil the mixture for 5 minutes, stirring often as it boils. Remove from the heat and stir in 2 packages (3-ounce size) Jello, any flavor. Stir until dissolved. While still hot, seal the conserve in sterilized jars. Once the jars are opened for use they must be kept refrigerated, as they do not keep well.

– Mamie Pickett

STRAWBERRY-RHUBARB JAM

Many an old miner's cabin — long abandoned — will still have rhubarb grow-

*...is the one plant that no
...seem to bother, and it thrives in
almost any climate.*

Finely chop 1 pound rhubarb. Crush 1 quart fresh strawberries. Combine the two fruits and measure 4 cups of the mixture into a large preserving kettle. Add 7 cups sugar. Place over high heat and bring to a boil. Boil 1 minute, stirring constantly. Remove from the heat and add ½ bottle of liquid pectin. Stir and skim for 5 minutes. Ladle into glasses and pour melted paraffin over the tops at once. This recipe should yield ten 6-ounce glasses of jam.   *– Mamie Pickett*

CANDIED RHUBARB PIE

Make a 9-inch pie shell but do not bake it. This is just the beginning for a super dessert. It's a rich one, so watch your waistline!

Combine 5 cups diced rhubarb, 1¼ cups sugar, 3 tablespoons flour, ¼ teaspoon salt, 2 tablespoons melted butter, and 1 beaten egg. Mix well and turn into the pie shell.

In a bowl combine ½ cup sugar, ½ cup flour, and ⅛ teaspoon salt. Cut in ¼ cup butter until the mixture resembles coarse cornmeal. Sprinkle over the top of the pie. Bake in a preheated

425°F. oven for 40 minutes. If the topping browns too fast, reduce the oven temperature to 375°F. to complete the baking.   *– Bekki Chapek*

MAT-SU POTATOES

The potatoes raised in the Matanuska and Susitna valleys may not be as famous in the South 48 as they are in Alaska, but they are much prized in our own state. Baked potatoes go well with innumerable entrées.

Choose 6 blemish-free potatoes of medium uniform size. Scrub the skins to make sure of cleanliness. Dry them and rub all over with a little margarine. Preheat the oven to 325°F. Prick each potato with a fork to provide vents. Place the potatoes on a cookie sheet. They will be easier to handle if all are on one pan rather than in the oven separately. Put the pan in the oven and bake for 1 hour. Protect your hand with a hot pad and squeeze the potatoes gently; if they "give" easily they are done. Otherwise continue cooking until they test done.

Remove the potatoes from the oven and cut a cross in the top of each. Squeeze the potato a little to open it up. Put a pat of margarine, salt, pepper, and snipped wild chives or bacon bits on the exposed part. Also, pass a bowl with softened margarine and the other seasonings creamed together in it so that more can be added to the potato as it is eaten.

HOMESTEAD HARVEST

The first green peas and new potatoes of the summer are a cause for celebration on the homestead. To enjoy them at their best they must be gathered and used right away — don't let them hang around in the refrigerator.

90

Often the new potatoes are not much bigger than large marbles when the first peas can be picked, but they are wonderful prepared this way. Do not peel the little nuggets — just scrape off their skins. Put them on to simmer in lightly salted water while you shell the peas. The peas can be cooked with the potatoes, but it is better if they are cooked separately. Put a little onion powder and salt in with the peas as they cook. The amount will depend on the quantity of peas. Cook the peas and potatoes until tender (it won't take long). We like these early vegetables drowned in White Sauce (p.91), but they are almost as good simply served with melted butter and any seasonings you like.

THE EXTRAORDINARY CARROT

Carrots are easy to raise. Just feed and water them well and keep them thinned so they will have room to grow. And they can be used in so many ways. Try the miniature species such as Little Finger.

Have you ever eaten carrot pie? It tastes almost like pumpkin pie. There is also carrot cake and carrot bread, and, of course, as a vegetable the carrot is king.

Besides using it all by itself, the carrot is excellent with peas, broccoli, cauliflower, Brussels sprouts, and cabbage. A stew wouldn't be complete without carrots, and neither would meat pie.

As if that were not enough to say in praise of the carrot, it has also been found to be one of the most healthful of foods. It is rich in minerals, vitamins, and fiber. Who could ask for more?

WHITE SAUCE

To make white sauce, which is called for in several places in this book, is a simple matter. If you are ambitious enough you might make a large batch of it and keep some on hand in the refrigerator for use now and again. The recipe below is for 1 cup of sauce.

Melt 2 tablespoons margarine or butter in a saucepan. Gradually stir in 1 tablespoon flour and keep stirring for a minute or two. Add 1 cup milk all at once and continue stirring. This should make a medium-thick sauce. Any seasonings you wish may then be added. We always use sea salt, black pepper, and a dash or two of onion powder. The rest depends on what we are using the sauce with.

CORN BREAD STUFFING

This is a good basic recipe for stuffing. Sometimes we add mushrooms or bacon bits, but usually we use it just as presented below. Chestnuts, sausage, oysters, cranberries, and corn can also be used to vary it.

Put some hot water and a largish lump of margarine in a small saucepan. The proportions of ingredients will depend on the amount of stuffing you are going to make. Add a little rice and some chopped onion when the water comes to a boil. We use Uncle Ben's brand, but any good brand will suffice. Reduce the heat and cook the rice, covered, until tender.

Meanwhile, cut into cubes or tear or crumble your bread. The secret to good stuffing, we think, is corn bread. We use from one-quarter to one-third as much corn bread as other bread. We often use several kinds of bread,

but all the bread should be stale and rather dry. Even croutons work well here. In a large bowl mix the bread with your choice of seasonings. A soup base of one kind or another, depending on what you are using the stuffing with, would be in order. Sage is always used in stuffing, and we use thyme, marjoram, and other such seasonings, too.

Pour the rice mixture over the bread and stir to mingle. Break 1 or 2 eggs over the lot and stir into the stuffing. If you prefer a loose dressing don't add too much liquid. We like ours packed in tight and solid, and that takes more liquid. Add more water if you think you need it. Put the stuffing in your fowl (or whatever you're stuffing) and pack any extra around it. Make plenty because it is good cold, too.

Sagewort (*Artemisia frigida*) is a northern plant that resembles the better-known commercial sage and that can be dried and used in place of sage. It is quite strong in flavor, so don't use too much.

MARINADE FOR WILD GAME

An all-purpose marinade for wild game, including wild fowl, is extremely useful. The following is one such recipe.

Put 2 cups lowbush cranberries through the food chopper using the finest blade. Pour the berries into a container more than large enough to hold the meat. Add 1 cup orange juice, a handful of chopped celery leaves, 1 raw apple, chopped (or the equivalent in applesauce), 3 or 4 cloves of garlic, crushed, and the same number of crushed peppercorns, 2 tablespoons dark brown sugar, and any other seasonings you care to use. Add enough water to cover the steaks or roast and stir to mingle the flavors. Marinate the meat (in the refrigerator or another cool place) from 3 to 24 hours, depending on the size of the meat and the age of the animal it came from. Remove the meat from the marinade and drain it in a colander for 20 minutes before cooking. The marinade can be used again if you don't wait too long.

ALL-PURPOSE MARINADE

Older fowl and moose or caribou that have lived beyond their appointed years sometimes need marinating for a few hours or even overnight. The recipe below should do for any such job.

Mix and stir vigorously for a minute or two the following ingredients: 1 cup wine vinegar, 1/2 cup soy sauce, 1 1/2 teaspoons salt, 1/4 teaspoon pepper, 1/4 teaspoon dried red pepper flakes, 1/2 teaspoon powdered ginger, 1 tablespoon dried minced onion, and 6 to 8 cloves of garlic, crushed. Immerse the meat in the marinade and turn occasionally. Ducks with a fishy odor, older birds, or other game should be marinated in this mixture for several hours or overnight. After marinating, drain the meat for an hour or so before cooking.

A cup of lowbush cranberry juice added to the above will hasten the marinating process and enhance the flavor, too.

TARTARE SAUCE FOR SEAFOOD

Commercially prepared tartare sauce can't compare with your own, and here is a simple way to make it.

Start with 1 cup good mayonnaise (homemade if you have it) and add 1 generous tablespoon each finely chopped stuffed olives and finely chopped onions and 2 tablespoons chopped sweet pickle. Stir to blend, then add 1 teaspoon prepared mustard. That is all there is to the sauce, and it is tops as an accompaniment for almost any seafood, either pan-fried or fried in deep fat. It is especially good with shellfish. Try it! You won't be sorry.

CREAM GRAVY

Cream steak gravy is a basic recipe and can be varied in many ways. You can use either cornstarch or flour as the thickening agent.

Pour out all but approximately 3 tablespoons of the fat in which the steak was pan-fried. If there is not that amount, just add a little margarine and allow it to melt. To the fat in the pan, add enough flour or cornstarch so that it will all be absorbed. (We like the flavor given by whole wheat flour.) Stir until the cornstarch or flour is absorbed and cook until it has browned a bit, stirring as it cooks. Then add 1 cup milk and cook over medium heat until the gravy comes to a boil. At this point, add 1 cup of your own home-frozen mushrooms and stir briskly until the gravy again comes to a boil. For a stronger meat flavor, add a teaspoon of beef soup base. If the gravy is too thick to please your family, gradually add more milk and cook gently between additions until it suits you.

This basic gravy is just a starting point. Instead of mushrooms, try dehydrated minced onions or peppers and experiment with herbs and other seasonings. A tablespoon or so of sherry is good, and a dash of a commercially prepared kitchen sauce adds a nice taste.

Items To Keep On Hand

Soup Bases (chicken, ham, and beef flavors), Crescent Mfg. Co., Seattle, WA.

Bouquet garni — little packets of seasonings to drop in soups, stews, etc. Walnut Acres, Penns Creek, PA. Send for catalog.

Homestead lemon — lemon-shaped plastic bottle containing lemon juice.

Bell pepper dices — red and green dried bell pepper pieces, Walnut Acres.

Potato Buds, Betty Crocker brand

Sea Salt — from the Mediterranean Sea

Minced dehydrated onion

Minced dried parsley

Minced dried chervil

Minced dried garlic

Garlic powder

Onion powder

Bacon bits (*not* the artificially flavored kind)

Crystallized ginger

Whole wheat flour

Brown sugar

Tomato purée in tubes

Canned mushrooms, stems and pieces

Jalapeño peppers, minced, dried, and canned

Dried red pepper flakes

Vegetable seasoning — dried and powdered vegetables good for all sorts of things, Walnut Acres.

Mixed dried vegetables — for soups, stews, goulash, etc. — Walnut Acres.

Herbs and spices to have on hand: nutmeg, cinnamon, ginger, cloves, mace, cumin, chili powder, black (and white) pepper, dry mustard, rosemary, basil, thyme, marjoram, cilantro (leaf coriander), oregano, bay leaves, curry powder, cayenne pepper, paprika (Hungarian), sage (rubbed), wild sage, etc.

Glossary

Barbecue — to roast over coals or in an oven, basting with highly seasoned sauce.

Baste — to moisten during cooking by drizzling liquid over meat.

Braise — to brown in a small amount of fat, adding a little liquid, covering tightly, and cooking slowly on top of the stove or in the oven.

Broil — to cook food by exposing directly to a heat source, such as a broiler or campfire.

Fricassee — to stew cut-up pieces of meat in gravy.

Fry — to cook in a small amount of fat. (See Sauté.) Deep-Fry — to fry in deep fat, usually heated to 375°F.

Marinade — the liquid in which meat is soaked to tenderize or flavor it.

Marinate — to soak or tenderize in a marinade.

Mince — to cut in very small pieces.

Pan-Broil — to cook uncovered in a hot skillet, without fat and pouring off fat as it fries out of the meat.

Parboil — to cook partially (more than just immersing) in boiling water.

Roast — to cook using dry heat, usually in an oven.

Sauté — to cook in a small amount of fat. (See Fry.)

Score — to cut parallel gashes partway through the surface of meat.

Simmer — to cook slowly over low heat.

Skewer — to fasten meat with wooden or metal pins so that it will hold its shape.

Steam — to cook by steam in either a pressure cooker or in a steamer made by placing a rack in the bottom of a kettle fitted with a tight cover.

Stew — to cook slowly and long in liquid on top of the stove.

Stock — concentrated liquid made by simmering meat or bones for a long time. Used as base for soups, gravies, and for basting and flavoring.

Please see *COOKING ALASKAN* by the Editors and Friends of ALASKA Magazine, published by Alaska Northwest Publishing Company, 130 Second Avenue South, Edmonds, Washington 98020 at $14.95 US dollars. This large-format cookbook covers in depth all of Alaska's edible resources in 500 pages. It is an excellent book and fun to read, as well as being chock-full of useful recipes. And, like the recipes in this booklet, the ones in *COOKING ALASKAN* can be adapted easily to ingredients from your local supermarket.